Digital Governance ... Municipalities Worldwide (2009)

A Longitudinal Assessment of Municipal Websites Throughout the World

Marc Holzer, Ph.D.
Dean, School of Public Affairs and Administration
Director, The E-Governance Institute,
The National Center for Public Performance
Rutgers, The State University of New Jersey, Campus at Newark

Min-Bong You, Ph.D.
Dean, Graduate School of Governance
Dean, College of Social Sciences
Sungkyunkwan University

Aroon Manoharan, Ph.D.
Assistant Professor of Public Administration
Department of Political Science, Kent State University
Associate Director, The E-Governance Institute

Project Co-Investigators at Rutgers University-Newark

Marc Fudge, Ph.D. Student, Rutgers University-Newark
Jessie Rumsey, Ph.D. Student, Kent State University
Min Ji Ha, Ph.D. Student, Sungkyunkwan University
Gautam Nayer, Ph.D., Assistant Professor,
Texas Southern University

Digital Governance in Municipalities Worldwide (2009)
A Longitudinal Assessment of Municipal Websites Throughout the World
©2010 Public Technology Institute

Published by:
Public Technology Institute
1426 Prince Street
Alexandria, Virginia 22314
www.pti.org

Printed in the United States of America
ISBN 1456363913
EAN-13 9781456363918

Contents

Acknowledgements

This volume, *Digital Governance in Municipalities Worldwide 2009*, was made possible through a collaboration between the E-Governance Institute at Rutgers, the State University of New Jersey, Campus at Newark and the Global e-Policy e-Government Institute at Sungkyunkwan University.

We are grateful for the work and assistance of research staffs in the E-Governance Institute, National Center for Public Performance at Rutgers, the State University of New Jersey, Campus at Newark and the Global e-Policy e-Government Institute at Sungkyunkwan University. Their enormous efforts and collaboration made this research successful.

We would like to express our thanks to the UN Division for Public Administration and Development Management (DPADM), for their continued support in this research.

Finally, we would also like to express our deepest thanks to the evaluators for their contributions in this project. Their participation truly makes the research project successful. On the following page we name our numerous evaluators of websites throughout the world as acknowledgement of their efforts.

2009 Digital Governance Evaluators

Jin Mi Ae	Kim Jungah	Fadi Salem
Dovile Alsauskaite	Jyldyz Kasymova	Satish Sampath
Colette Apelian	Meelis Kitsing	Dr. Nur Sat
Thomas Arndt	Simon Knutsson	Jenna Scheps
Itai Beeri	Mateja Kunstelj	Susan Schweigert
Mauricio Benavides	Olena Yanakova-Lange	Olena Shchegel
Helena Buric	Edina Leiher	Fidaa Shehada
Ibrahim Ahmed Elbadawi	Yuguo Liao	Hannes Sonnsjo
Vuk Èomiæ	Nevena Manic	Stephen Spacek
Simon Wolfgang Fuchs	Sylvia Mlynarska	Alena Srankova
Mariana Giraudo	Kim Ngan Le Nguyen	Reima Suomi
Marion Greene	Ernest Nino-Murcia	Efthimios Tambouris
Laura Gutierrez	Cezara Nanu	Zoran Tatarchevski
Emily Hagstrom	Jelena Novakovic	Jaganathan Vadivel
Ghazwan Hassna	Makiko Oku	Arturas Vedrickas
Lizbeth Herrera	Fernanda Martinez	Olesya Vodenicharska
Kim Hyung Hoon	Milton Alfonso Ortega	Tatjana Zagare-Vitins
Nguyen Dang Hung	Larisa Ozols	Jung Min-young
Cho il hyoung	Ana Pantelic	Wenxuan Yu
Ju Hee Jin	Gennadi Poberezny	
Frans Jorna	David Reyero	

Executive Summary

The Digital Governance in Municipalities Worldwide Survey assessed the practice of digital governance in large municipalities worldwide in 2009. This research, replicating our continuing surveys in 2003, 2005 and 2007, evaluated the websites of municipalities in terms of digital governance and ranked them on a global scale. Simply stated, digital governance includes both digital government (delivery of public service) and digital democracy (citizen participation in governance). Specifically, we analyzed security, usability, and content of websites, the type of online services currently being offered, and citizen response and participation through websites established by municipal governments (Holzer & Kim, 2007).

The methodology of the 2009 survey of municipal websites throughout the world mirrors our previous research in 2003, 2005 and 2007. This research focused on cities throughout the world based on their population size and the total number of individuals using the Internet in each nation. The top 100 most wired nations were identified using data from the International Telecommunication Union (ITU), an organization affiliated with the United Nations (UN). The largest city by population in each of these 100 countries was then selected for the study and used as a surrogate for all cities in the respective country.

To examine how the local populations perceive their government online, the study evaluated the official websites of each of these largest cities in their native languages. Of the 100 cities selected, 87 cities were found to have official municipal websites, and these were evaluated between July 2009 and December 2009. For the 2005 survey, 81 of the 100 cities had official websites, which increased to 86 for the 2007 survey and 87 for the 2009 survey. This represents a significant increase in the adoption of e-governance among municipalities across the world.

Our instrument for evaluating city and municipal websites consisted of five components: 1. Security and Privacy; 2. Usability; 3. Content; 4. Services; and 5. Citizen Participation. For each of those five components, our research applied 18-20 measures, and each measure was coded on a scale of four-points (0, 1, 2, 3) or a dichotomy of two-points (0, 3 or 0, 1). Furthermore, in developing an overall score for each municipality we have equally weighted each of the five categories so as not to skew the research in favor of a particular category (regardless of the number of questions in each category). This reflects the same methods utilized in the previous studies. To ensure reliability, each municipal website was assessed in the native language by two evaluators, and in cases where significant variation (+ or − 10%) existed on the adjusted score between evaluators, websites were analyzed a third time.

Based on the 2009 evaluation of 87 cities, Seoul, Prague, Hong Kong, New York, and Singapore represent the cities with the highest evaluation scores. There were noticeable changes in the top five cities when compared to the 2007 study. Seoul remained the highest ranked city, and the gap between first and second had slightly increased. In some cases, the scores may have slightly declined from the previous study. Table 1 lists the top 20 municipalities in digital governance 2005 through 2009, with Table 2 listing the 20 municipalities from the 2009 study along with their scores in individual categories. Tables 3 to Table 7 represent the top ranking municipalities in each of the five categories.

Table 1. *Top Cities in Digital Governance 2005–2009*

	2005		2007		2009	
Rank	City	Score	City	Score	City	Score
1	Seoul	81.70	Seoul	87.74	Seoul	84.74
2	New York	72.71	Hong Kong	71.24	Prague	72.84
3	Shanghai	63.93	Helsinki	71.01	Hong Kong	62.83
4	Hong Kong	61.51	Singapore	68.56	New York	61.10
5	Sydney	60.82	Madrid	67.98	Singapore	58.81
6	Singapore	60.22	London	65.79	Shanghai	57.41
7	Tokyo	59.24	Tokyo	59.89	Madrid	55.59
8	Zurich	55.99	Bangkok	59.01	Vienna	55.48
9	Toronto	55.1	New York	56.54	Auckland	55.28
10	Riga	53.95	Vienna	53.99	Toronto	52.87
11	Warsaw	53.26	Dublin	53.38	Paris	52.65
12	Reykjavik	52.24	Toronto	51.99	Bratislava	52.51
13	Sofia	49.11	Berlin	51.36	London	51.96
14	Prague	47.27	Zurich	51.02	Jerusalem	50.64
15	Luxembourg	46.58	Prague	50.34	Tokyo	50.59
16	Amsterdam	46.44	Buenos Aires	49.89	Zagreb	50.16
17	Paris	45.49	Bratislava	49.82	Ljubljana	49.39
18	Macao	45.48	Sydney	48.60	Lisbon	48.82
19	Dublin	44.10	Amsterdam	47.72	Brussels	48.01
20	Bratislava	43.65	Rome	46.98	Johannesburg	47.68

Table 2. *Top 20 Cities in Digital Governance (2009)*

Rank	City	Overall	Privacy	Usability	Content	Services	Partici-pation
1	Seoul	84.74	18.80	17.50	18.20	19.15	11.09
2	Prague	72.84	16.70	17.62	13.02	13.86	11.64
3	Hong Kong	62.83	11.20	15.31	14.40	13.56	8.36
4	New York	61.10	12.80	13.44	13.80	15.42	5.64
5	Singapore	58.81	6.40	16.88	9.60	15.93	10.00
6	Shanghai	57.41	11.20	11.25	10.00	14.41	10.55
7	Madrid	55.59	11.20	14.38	13.20	13.90	2.91
8	Vienna	55.48	16.00	11.88	12.80	6.44	8.36
9	Auckland	55.28	10.40	14.38	16.80	6.07	7.64
10	Toronto	52.87	12.80	13.00	12.40	8.85	5.82
11	Paris	52.65	12.00	13.13	12.40	7.12	8.00
12	Bratislava	52.51	13.60	17.50	9.20	7.12	5.09
13	London	51.96	13.60	15.00	8.80	9.83	4.73
14	Jerusalem	50.64	8.80	15.63	13.60	11.53	1.09
15	Tokyo	50.59	8.00	14.25	12.40	10.85	5.09
16	Zagreb	50.16	9.60	13.00	12.80	7.12	7.64
17	Ljubljana	49.39	8.00	13.13	11.60	10.85	5.82
18	Lisbon	48.82	8.80	15.00	10.80	9.49	4.73
19	Brussels	48.01	12.00	16.25	11.60	7.07	1.09
20	Johannes-burg	47.68	4.00	16.25	8.80	8.81	9.82

Table 3. *Top 10 Cities in Privacy and Security (2009)*

Rank	City	Country	Privacy
1	Seoul	Republic of Korea	18.80
2	Prague	Czech Republic	16.70
3	Vienna	Austria	16.00
4	Ho Chi Minh City	Vietnam	14.40
5	Bratislava	Slovakia	13.60
5	London	UK	13.60
5	Dubai	UAE	13.60
8	New York	USA	12.80
8	Toronto	Canada	12.80
8	Berlin	Germany	12.80
8	Sydney	Australia	12.80

Table 4. *Top 10 Cities in Usability (2009)*

Rank	City	Country	Usability
1	Prague	Czech Republic	17.62
2	Seoul	Republic of Korea	17.50
2	Bratislava	Slovakia	17.50
4	Singapore	Singapore	16.88
4	Cairo	Egypt	16.88
6	Brussels	Belgium	16.25
6	Johannesburg	South Africa	16.25
6	Bangkok	Thailand	16.25
9	Jerusalem	Israel	15.63
9	Sao Paulo	Brazil	15.63
9	Copenhagen	Denmark	15.63
9	Bucharest	Romania	15.63

Table 5. *Top 10 Cities in Content (2009)*

Rank	City	Country	Content
1	Seoul	Republic of Korea	18.20
2	Auckland	New Zealand	16.80
3	Tallinn	Estonia	16.40
4	Hong Kong	Hong Kong	14.40
5	New York	USA	13.80
6	Jerusalem	Israel	13.60
7	Madrid	Spain	13.20
7	Helsinki	Finland	13.20
9	Prague	Czech Republic	13.02
10	Vienna	Austria	12.80
10	Zagreb	Croatia	12.80
10	Oslo	Norway	12.80
10	Santa Fé de Bogotá	Colombia	12.80

Table 6. *Top 10 Cities in Service Delivery (2009)*

Rank	City	Country	Services
1	Seoul	Republic of Korea	19.15
2	Singapore	Singapore	15.93
3	New York	USA	15.42
4	Shanghai	China	14.41
5	Madrid	Spain	13.90
6	Prague	Czech Republic	13.86
7	Hong Kong	Hong Kong	13.56
8	Mexico City	Mexico	12.88
9	Tallinn	Estonia	12.20
10	Jerusalem	Israel	11.53

Table 7. *Top 10 Cities in Citizen Participation (2009)*

Rank	City	Country	Participation
1	Mexico City	Mexico	13.45
2	Prague	Czech Republic	11.64
3	Bangkok	Thailand	11.27
4	Seoul	Republic of Korea	11.09
5	Shanghai	China	10.55
6	Singapore	Singapore	10.00
7	Johannesburg	South Africa	9.82
8	Vienna	Austria	8.36
8	Hong Kong	Hong Kong	8.36
10	Paris	France	8.00

The average score for digital governance in municipalities throughout the world is 35.93, an increase from 33.37 in 2007, 33.11 in 2005 and 28.49 in 2003. The average score for municipalities in OECD countries is 46.69, while the average score in non-OECD countries is 30.83. Our 2007 research indicated a divide in terms of digital governance throughout the world, but in 2009 the divide appears to have been slightly bridged. Among the OECD and non-OECD countries, the digital gap between the two scores increased from 12.08 in 2003 to 17.85 in 2005, but decreased to 17.54 in 2007 and 15.86 in 2009. However, more needs to be done in non-OECD countries to bridge the divide, and it is very important for international organizations such as the UN and cities in advanced countries to assist in this effort.

This research represents a continued effort to evaluate digital governance in large municipalities throughout the world. The continued study of municipalities worldwide, with the next Worldwide Survey planned in 2011, will further provide insights into the direction and the performance of e-governance throughout regions of the world.

CHAPTER 1

Introduction

This research replicates surveys completed in 2003, 2005 and 2007, and evaluates the practice of digital governance in large municipalities worldwide in 2009. The following chapters represent the overall findings of the research. Chapter 2 outlines the methodology utilized in determining the websites evaluated, as well as the instrument used in the evaluations. The methodological steps taken by the 2009 survey of municipal websites mirrors those of the previous research done in 2007. Our survey instrument uses 98 measures and we use a rigorous approach for conducting the evaluations. Chapter 3 presents the overall findings for the 2009 evaluation. The overall results are also broken down into results by continents, and by OECD and non-OECD member countries.

Chapter 4 provides a longitudinal assessment of the 2007 and 2009 evaluations, with comparisons among continents, e-governance categories and OECD and non-OECD member countries. Chapters 5 through 9 take a closer look at the results for each of the five e-governance categories. Chapter 5 focuses on the results of privacy and security with regard to municipal websites. Chapter 6 looks at the usability of municipalities throughout the world. Chapter 7 presents the findings for Content, while Chapter 8 looks at Services. Chapter 9 concludes the focus of specific e-governance categories by presenting the findings of citizen participation online.

Chapter 10 takes a closer look at the best practices, and the report concludes with Chapter 11, providing recommendations and discussion of significant findings.

CHAPTER 2

Methodology

The methodological steps taken by the 2009 survey of municipal websites throughout the world mirror the previous research done in 2007, 2005 and 2003. The following review of our methodology borrows from our Digital Governance (2007) report based on the 2007 data. The methodology of the 2009 survey of municipal websites throughout the world involves the same 98-measure Rutgers Survey Index, along with some changes in the cities selected. This research focused on cities throughout the world based on their population size and the total number of individuals using the Internet in each nation. These cities were identified using data from the International Telecommunication Union (ITU), an organization affiliated with the United Nations (UN). The top 100 most wired nations were identified using information on the total number of online users, obtained from the ITU-UN. The largest city, by population in each of these 100 countries was then selected for the study, as a surrogate for all cities in a particular country.

The rationale for selecting the largest municipalities stems from the e-governance literature, which suggests a positive relationship between population and e-governance capacity at the local level (Moon, 2002; Moon and deLeon, 2001; Musso, et. al., 2000; Weare, et. al. 1999). The study evaluated the official websites of each of these largest cities in their native languages. Of the 100 cities selected, 87 cities were found to have official websites and these were evaluated from July 2009 to December 2009. For the 2007 survey, 86 of the 100 cities had official websites, which increased from 81 for the 2005 survey. This represents a significant increase in the adoption of e-governance among municipalities across the world. Table 2-1 (see next page) is a list of the 100 cities selected.

Website Survey

In this research, the main city homepage is defined as the official website where information about city administration and online services are provided by the city. Municipalities across the world are increasingly developing websites to provide their services online; however, e-government is more than simply constructing a website. The emphasis should be more focused on using such technologies to effectively provide government services. According to Pardo (2000), some of the initiatives in this direction are:

1) providing 24 x 7 access to government information and public meetings; 2) providing mechanisms to enable citizens to comply with state and federal rules regarding drivers licenses, business licenses, etc.; 3) providing access to special benefits like welfare funds and pensions; 4) providing a network across various government agencies to enable collaborative approaches to serving citizens; and 5) providing various channels for digital democracy and citizen participation initiatives.

Table 2-1. *100 Cities Selected by Continent (2009)*

AFRICA (16)	
Abidjan (Côte d'Ivoire)	Harare (Zimbabwe)*
Accra (Ghana)	Kampala (Uganda)
Algiers (Algeria)*	Omdurman (Sudan)*
Cairo (Egypt)	Lagos (Nigeria)
Cape Town (South Africa)	Luanda (Angola)*
Casablanca (Morocco)	Lusaka (Zambia)
Dakar (Senegal)	Nairobi (Kenya)
Douala (Cameroon)*	Tunis (Tunisia)
ASIA (27)	
Almaty (Kazakhstan)	Karachi (Pakistan)
Amman (Jordan)	Kuala Lumpur (Malaysia)
Baku (Azerbaijan)	Kuwait City (Kuwait)
Bangkok (Thailand)	Mumbai (India)
Beirut (Lebanon)	Quezon City (Philippines)
Bishkek (Kyrgyzstan)*	Riyadh (Saudi Arabia)
Colombo (Sri Lanka)	Seoul (Republic of Korea)
Damascus (Syria)*	Shanghai (China)
Dubai (United Arab Emirates)	Singapore (Singapore)
Ho Chi Minh City (Vietnam)	Tashkent (Uzbekistan)
Hong Kong (Hong Kong)	Tehran (Iran)
Jakarta (Indonesia)	Tokyo (Japan)
Jerusalem (Israel)	

EUROPE (36)	
Amsterdam (Netherlands)	Minsk (Belarus)
Athens (Greece)	Moscow (Russian Federation)
Belgrade (Serbia and Montenegro)	Oslo (Norway)
Berlin (Germany)	Paris (France)
Bratislava (Slovak Republic)	Prague (Czech Republic)
Brussels (Belgium)	Riga (Latvia)
Bucharest (Romania)	Rome (Italy)
Budapest (Hungary)	Sarajevo (Bosnia and Herzegovina)
Chisinau (Moldova)	Sofia (Bulgaria)
Copenhagen (Denmark)	Skopje (TFYR Macedonia)
Dublin (Ireland)	Stockholm (Sweden)
Helsinki (Finland)	Tallinn (Estonia)
Istanbul (Turkey)	Vienna (Austria)
Kiev (Ukraine)	Vilnius (Lithuania)
Lisbon (Portugal)	Warsaw (Poland)
Ljubljana (Slovenia)	Zagreb (Croatia)
London (United Kingdom)	Zurich (Switzerland)
Madrid (Spain)	
NORTH AMERICA (10)	
Guatemala City (Guatemala)	San Jose (Costa Rica)
Havana (Cuba)*	San Juan (Puerto Rico)
Kingston (Jamaica)*	San Salvador (El Salvador)
Mexico City (Mexico)	Santo Domingo (Dominican Republic)
New York (United States)	Tegucigalpa (Honduras)*
Panama City (Panama)	Toronto (Canada)
Port-au-Prince (Haiti)*	
SOUTH AMERICA (9)	
Buenos Aires (Argentina)	Montevideo (Uruguay)
Caracas (Venezuela)	Santa Fe De Bogota (Colombia)
Guayaquil (Ecuador)	Santiago (Chile)
La Paz (Bolivia)	Sao Paulo (Brazil)
Lima (Peru)	
OCEANIA (2)	
Auckland (New Zealand)	Sydney (Australia)

* *Official city websites unavailable*

The city website includes information about the city council, mayor and executive branch. If there are separate homepages for agencies, departments, or the city council, evaluators examined if these sites were linked to the menu on the main city homepage. If the website was not linked, it was excluded from evaluation.

E-Governance Survey Instrument

The Rutgers E-Governance Survey Instrument is the most comprehensive index in practice for e-governance research today. With 98 measures and five distinct categorical areas of e-governance research, the survey instrument is unlike any other. Our instrument for evaluating municipal websites consists of five components: 1. Security and Privacy; 2. Usability; 3. Content; 4. Services; and 5. Citizen Participation. Table 2-2 summarizes the 2009 survey instrument, and Appendix A presents an overview of the criteria.

Table 2-2. *E-Governance Performance Measures*

E-governance Category	Key Concepts	Raw Score	Weighted Score	Keywords
Security/ Privacy	18	25	20	Privacy policies, authentication, encryption, data management, cookies
Usability	20	32	20	User-friendly design, branding, length of homepage, targeted audience links or channels, and site search capabilities
Content	20	48	20	Access to current accurate information, public documents, reports, publications, and multimedia materials
Service	20	59	20	Transactional services—purchase or register, interaction between citizens, businesses and government
Citizen Participation	20	55	20	Online civic engagement/ policy deliberation, citizen based performance measurement
Total	98	219	100	

The following section highlights the specific design of our survey instrument, which utilizes 98 measures, of which 43 are dichotomous. For each of the five e-governance components, our research applies 18 to 20 measures, and for questions, which were not dichotomous, each measure was coded on a four-point scale (0, 1, 2, 3; see Table 2-3 below). Furthermore, in developing an overall score for each municipality, we have equally weighted each of the five categories so as not to skew the research in favor of a particular category (regardless of the number of questions in each category). The dichotomous measures in the "service" and "citizen participation" categories correspond with values on a four-point scale of "0" or "3"; dichotomous measures in "privacy" or "usability" correspond to ratings of "0" or "1" on the scale.

Table 2-3. *E-Governance Scale*

Scale	Description
0	Information about a given topic does not exist on the website
1	Information about a given topic exists on the website (including links to other information and e-mail addresses)
2	Downloadable items are available on the website (forms, audio, video, and other one-way transactions, popup boxes)
3	Services, transactions, or interactions can take place completely online (credit card transactions, applications for permits, searchable databases, use of cookies, digital signatures, restricted access)

Our instrument placed a higher value on some dichotomous measures, due to the relative value of the different e-government services being evaluated. For example, evaluators using our instrument in the "service" category were given the option of scoring websites as either a "0" or "3" when assessing whether a site allowed users to access private information online (e.g. educational records, medical records, point total of driving violations, lost property). "No access" equated to a rating of "0." Allowing residents or employees to access private information online was a higher order task that required more technical competence, and was clearly an online service, or "3," as defined in Table 2-3.

However, when assessing a site as to whether or not it had a privacy statement or policy, evaluators were given the choice of scoring the site as "0" or "1." The presence or absence of a security policy was clearly a content issue that emphasized placing information online, and corresponded with a value of "1" on the scale outlined in Table 2-3. The differential values assigned to dichotomous categories were useful in comparing the different components of municipal websites with one another.

To ensure reliability, each municipal website was assessed by two evaluators, and in cases where significant variation (+ or – 10%) existed on the weighted score between evaluators, websites were analyzed a third time. Furthermore, an example for each measure indicated how to score the variable. Evaluators were also given comprehensive written instructions for assessing websites.

E-Governance Categories

This section details the five e-governance categories and discusses specific measures that were used to evaluate websites. The discussion of security and privacy examines privacy policies and issues related to authentication. Discussion of the Usability category involves traditional web pages, forms and search tools. The Content category is addressed in terms of access to contact information, access to public documents and disability access, as well as access to multimedia and time sensitive information. The section on services examines interactive services, services that allow users to purchase or pay for services, and the ability of users to apply or register for municipal events or services online. Finally, the measures for citizen participation involve examining how local governments are engaging citizens and providing mechanisms for citizens to participate in government online.

Security/Privacy

The first part of our analysis examined the security and privacy of municipal websites in two key areas, privacy policies and authentication of users. In examining municipal privacy policies, we determined whether such a policy was available on every page that accepted data, and whether or not the word "privacy" was used in the link to such a statement. In addition, we looked for privacy policies on every page that required or accepted data. We were also interested in determining if privacy policies identified the agencies collecting the information, and whether the policy identified exactly what data was being collected on the site.

Our analysis checked to see if the intended use of the data was explicitly stated on the website. The analysis examined whether the privacy policy addressed the use or sale of data collected on the website by outside or third party organizations. Our research also determined if there was an option to decline the disclosure of personal information to third parties. This included other municipal agencies, other state and local government offices, or businesses in the private sector. Furthermore, we examined privacy policies to determine if third party agencies or organizations were governed by the same privacy policies as was the municipal website. We also determined whether users had the ability to review personal data records and contest inaccurate or incomplete information.

In examining factors affecting the security and privacy of local government websites, we addressed managerial measures that limit access of data and assure that it is not used for unauthorized purposes. The use of encryption in the transmission of data, as well as the storage of personal information on secure servers, was also examined. We also determined if websites used digital signatures to authenticate users. In assessing how or whether municipalities used their websites to authenticate users, we examined whether public or private information was accessible through a restricted area that required a password and/or registration.

A growing e-governance trend at the local level is for municipalities to offer their website users access to public, and in some cases private, information online. Other research has discussed the governance issues associated with sites that choose to charge citizens for access to public information (West, 2001). We add our own concerns about the impact of the digital divide if public records are available only through the Internet or if municipalities insist on charging a fee for access to public records. Our analysis specifically addresses online access to public databases by determining if public information such as property tax assessments, is available to users of municipal websites. In addition, there are concerns that public agencies will use their websites to monitor citizens or create profiles based on the information they access online. For example, many websites use "cookies" or "web beacons" to customize their websites for users, but that technology can also be used to monitor Internet habits and profile visitors to websites. Our analysis examined municipal privacy policies to determine if they addressed the use of cookies or web beacons.

Usability

This research also examined the usability of municipal websites. Simply stated, we wanted to know if sites were "user friendly." To address usability concerns, we adopted several best practices and measures from other public and private sector research (Giga, 2000). Our analysis of usability examined three types of websites: traditional web pages, forms, and search tools.

To evaluate traditional web pages written using hypertext markup language (html), we examined issues such as branding and structure (e.g. consistent color, font, graphics, page length etc.). For example, we looked to see if all pages used consistent color, formatting, "default colors" (e.g. blue links and purple visited links) and underlined text to indicate links. Other items examined included whether system hardware and software requirements were clearly stated on the website.

In addition, our research examined each municipality's homepage to determine if it was too long (two or more screen lengths) or if alternative versions of long documents, such as .pdf or .doc files, were available. The use of targeted audience links or "channels" to customize the website for specific groups such as citizens, businesses, or other public agencies was also examined. We looked for the consistent use of navigation bars and links to the homepage on every page.

The availability of a "sitemap" or hyperlinked outline of the entire website was examined. Our assessment also examined whether duplicated link names connect to the same content.

Our research examined online forms to determine their usability in submitting data or conducting searches of municipal websites. We looked at issues such as whether field labels aligned appropriately with field, whether fields were accessible by keystrokes (e.g. tabs), or whether the cursor was automatically placed in the first field. We also examined whether required fields were noted explicitly, and whether the tab order of fields was logical. For example, after a user filled out their first name and pressed the "tab" key, did the cursor automatically go to the surname field? Or, did the page skip to another field such as zip code, only to return to the surname later?

We also checked to see if form pages provided additional information about how to fix errors if they were submitted. For example, did users have to reenter information if errors were submitted, or did the site flag incomplete or erroneous forms before accepting them? Also, did the site give a confirmation page after a form was submitted, or did it return users to the homepage?

Our analysis also addressed the use of search tools on municipal websites. We examined sites to determine if help was available for searching a municipality's website, or if the scope of searches could be limited to specific areas of the site. Were users able to search only in "public works" or "the mayor's office," or did the search tool always search the entire site? We also looked for advanced search features such as exact phrase searching, the ability to match all/ any words, and Boolean searching capabilities (e.g. the ability to use AND/OR/NOT operators). Our analysis also addressed a site's ability to sort search results by relevance or other criteria.

Content

Content is a critical component of any website. No matter how technologically advanced a website's features, if its content is not current, if it is difficult to navigate, or if the information provided is not correct, then it is not fulfilling its purpose. When examining website content, our research examined five key areas: access to contact information, public documents, disability access, multimedia materials, and time sensitive information. When addressing contact information, we looked for information about each agency represented on the website.

In addition, we also looked for the availability of office hours or a schedule of when agency offices are open. In assessing the availability of public documents, we looked for the availability of the municipal code or charter online. We also looked for content items, such as agency mission statements and minutes of public meetings. Other content items included access to budget information and publications. Our assessment also examined whether websites provided access to disabled users through either "bobby compliance" (disability access for the blind, http://www.cast.org/bobby) or disability access for deaf users via a TDD phone service. We also checked to see if sites offered content in more than one language.

Time sensitive information that was examined included the use of a municipal website for emergency management, and the use of a website as an alert mechanism (e.g. terrorism alert or severe weather alert). We also checked for time sensitive information such as the posting of job vacancies or a calendar of community events. In addressing the use of multimedia, we examined each site to determine if audio or video files of public events, speeches, or meetings were available.

Services

A critical component of e-governance is the provision of municipal services online. Our analysis examined two different types of services: (1) those that allow citizens to interact with the municipality, and (2) services that allow users to register for municipal events or services online. In many cases, municipalities have developed the capacity to accept payment for municipal services and taxes. The first type of service examined, which implies interactivity, can be as basic as forms that allow users to request information or file complaints. Local governments across the world use advanced interactive services to allow users to report crimes or violations, customize municipal homepages based on their needs (e.g. portal customization), and access private information online, such as court records, education records, or medical records. Our analysis examined municipal websites to determine if such interactive services were available.

The second type of service examined in this research determined if municipalities have the capacity to allow citizens to register for municipal services online. For example, many jurisdictions now allow citizens to apply for permits and licenses online. Online permitting can be used for services that vary from building permits to dog licenses. In addition, some local governments are using the Internet for procurement, allowing potential contractors to access requests for proposals or even bid for municipal contracts online. In other cases, local governments are chronicling the procurement process by listing the total number of bidders for a contract online, and in some cases listing contact information for bidders.

This analysis also examined municipal websites to determine if they developed the capacity to allow users to purchase or pay for municipal services and fees online. Examples of transactional services from across the United States include the payment of public utility bills and parking tickets online. In many jurisdictions, cities and municipalities allow online users to file or pay local taxes, or pay fines such as traffic tickets. In some cases, cities around the world are allowing their users to register or purchase tickets to events in city halls or arenas online.

Citizen Participation

Finally, online citizen participation in government continues to be the most recent area of e-governance study. As noted in the 2003 survey, the Internet is a convenient mechanism for citizen-users to engage their government, and also because of the potential to decentralize decision-making. We have strengthened our survey instrument in the area of Citizen Participation and once again found that the potential for online participation is still in its early stages of development. Very few public agencies offer online opportunities for civic engagement. Our analysis looked at several ways public agencies at the local level were involving citizens. For example, do municipal websites allow users to provide online comments or feedback to individual agencies or elected officials?

Our analysis examined whether local governments offer current information about municipal governance online or through an online newsletter or e-mail listserv. Our analysis also examined the use of internet-based polls about specific local issues. In addition, we examined whether communities allow users to participate and view the results of citizen satisfaction surveys online. For example, some municipalities used their websites to measure performance and published the results of performance measurement activities online.

Still other municipalities used online bulletin boards or other chat capabilities for gathering input on public issues. Online bulletin boards offer citizens the opportunity to post ideas, comments, or opinions without specific discussion topics. In some cases agencies attempt to structure online discussions around policy issues or specific agencies. Our research looked for municipal use of the Internet to foster civic engagement and citizen participation in government.

CHAPTER 3

Overall Results

The following chapter presents the results for all the evaluated municipal websites during 2009. Table 3-1 provides the rankings for 87 municipal websites and their overall scores. The overall scores reflect the combined scores of each municipality's score in the five e-governance component categories. The highest possible score for any one city website is 100. Seoul received a score of 84.74, the highest ranked city website for 2009. Seoul's website was also the highest ranked in 2007, 2005 and 2003 with scores of 87.74, 81.70 and 73.48. Prague had the second highest ranked municipal website, with a score 72.84, moving up significantly from its fifteenth place ranking in 2007. Hong Kong ranked third with a score of 62.83 in 2009 and New York and Singapore complete the top five ranked municipal websites with scores of 61.10 and 58.81, respectively. The results of the overall rankings are separated by continent in Tables 3-2 through 3-7. The top ranked cities for each continent are Johannesburg (Africa), Seoul (Asia), Prague (Europe), New York City (North America), Sydney (Oceania) and Sao Paolo (South America). Prague replaced Helsinki as the highest ranked city for European municipalities and Sao Paulo switched places with Buenos Aires as the highest ranked city in South America. Also included in the rankings by continent are the scores for each of the five e-governance component categories.

Table 3-1. *Overall E-Governance Rankings (2009)*

Rank	City	Country	Score
1	Seoul	Republic of Korea	84.74
2	Prague	Czech Republic	72.84
3	Hong Kong	Hong Kong	62.83
4	New York	USA	61.10
5	Singapore	Singapore	58.81
6	Shanghai	China	57.41
7	Madrid	Spain	55.59
8	Vienna	Austria	55.48
9	Auckland	New Zealand	55.28

Table 3-1. *Continued*

Rank	City	Country	Score
10	Toronto	Canada	52.87
11	Paris	France	52.65
12	Bratislava	Slovakia	52.51
13	London	UK	51.96
14	Jerusalem	Israel	50.64
15	Tokyo	Japan	50.59
16	Zagreb	Croatia	50.16
17	Ljubljana	Slovenia	49.39
18	Lisbon	Portugal	48.82
19	Brussels	Belgium	48.01
20	Johannesburg	South Africa	47.68
21	Vilnius	Lithuania	47.50
22	Ho Chi Minh City	Vietnam	47.12
23	Tehran	Iran	46.17
24	Sao Paulo	Brazil	45.98
25	Kuala Lumpur	Malaysia	45.87
26	Helsinki	Finland	45.61
27	Dublin	Ireland	45.16
28	Oslo	Norway	44.76
29	Bangkok	Thailand	44.40
30	Buenos Aires	Argentina	43.59
31	Mexico City	Mexico	43.04
32	Berlin	Germany	42.90
33	Sydney	Australia	41.91
34	Stockholm	Sweden	41.79
35	Warsaw	Poland	41.66
36	Tallinn	Estonia	41.57
37	Moscow	Russia	40.10
38	Santa Fé de Bogotá	Colombia	37.85
39	Copenhagen	Denmark	37.78
40	Riga	Latvia	36.88
41	Montevideo	Uruguay	35.02
42	Bucharest	Romania	34.65

43	Amsterdam	Netherlands	34.27
44	Dubai	UAE	33.14
45	Sofia	Bulgaria	33.13
46	Jakarta	Indonesia	32.70
47	Zurich	Switzerland	32.65
48	Mumbai	India	32.58
49	Tunis	Tunisia	32.05
50	Cairo	Egypt	31.83
51	Istanbul	Turkey	30.93
52	Almaty	Kazakhstan	30.56
53	Lima	Peru	29.76
54	Amman	Jordan	29.11
55	Belgrade	Serbia	28.65
56	Santo Domingo	Dominican Republic	27.70
57	Rome	Italy	26.85
58	Riyadh	Saudi Arabia	26.79
59	Skopje	Macedonia	26.56
60	San Jose	Costa Rica	25.57
61	Guayaquil	Ecuador	25.47
62	Kiev	Ukraine	25.45
63	Minsk	Belarus	25.40
64	Athens	Greece	24.84
65	Budapest	Hungary	24.76
66	Santiago	Chile	24.08
67	Quezon City	Philippines	23.99
68	Casablanca	Morocco	22.39
69	Guatemala City	Guatemala	21.56
70	Colombo	Sri Lanka	21.40
71	Panama City	Panama	20.94
71	Lagos	Nigeria	20.94
73	Karachi	Pakistan	20.88
74	San Juan	Puerto Rico	20.53
75	San Salvador	El Salvador	20.52
76	Chisinau	Moldova	20.31
77	Kuwait City	Kuwait	19.96

Table 3-1. *Continued*

Rank	City	Country	Score
78	Santa Cruz	Bolivia	19.94
79	Caracas	Venezuela	19.33
80	Lusaka	Zambia	19.02
81	Kampala	Uganda	17.69
82	Beirut	Lebanon	16.75
83	Accra	Ghana	14.28
84	Sarajevo	Bosnia and Herzegovina	12.26
85	Nairobi	Kenya	10.61
86	Tashkent	Uzbekistan	9.78
87	Baku	Azerbaijan	7.78

Table 3-2. *Results of Evaluation in African Cities (2009)*

Rank	City	Score	Privacy	Usability	Content	Services	Partici- pation
1	Johannes- burg	47.68	47.68	4.00	16.25	8.80	8.81
2	Tunis	32.05	32.05	0.00	15.00	7.60	5.08
3	Cairo	31.83	31.83	2.40	16.88	8.00	2.37
4	Casablanca	22.39	22.39	2.40	11.25	5.60	1.69
5	Lagos	20.94	20.94	4.80	5.00	8.40	2.37
6	Lusaka	19.02	19.02	2.40	6.25	4.80	3.39
7	Kampala	17.69	17.69	2.40	10.00	3.60	1.69
8	Accra	14.28	14.28	0.00	6.25	2.80	3.05
9	Nairobi	10.61	2.40	6.25	1.60	0.00	0.36

Table 3-3. *Results of Evaluation in Asian Cities (2009)*

Rank	City	Score	Privacy	Usability	Content	Services	Partici-pation
1	Seoul	84.74	18.80	17.50	18.20	19.15	11.09
2	Hong Kong	62.83	11.20	15.31	14.40	13.56	8.36
3	Singapore	58.81	6.40	16.88	9.60	15.93	10.00
4	Shanghai	57.41	11.20	11.25	10.00	14.41	10.55
5	Jerusalem	50.64	8.80	15.63	13.60	11.53	1.09
6	Tokyo	50.59	8.00	14.25	12.40	10.85	5.09
7	Ho Chi Minh City	47.12	14.40	15.00	9.20	7.80	0.73
8	Tehran	46.17	12.56	13.75	8.20	7.46	4.20
9	Kuala Lumpur	45.87	10.40	11.88	9.40	9.46	4.73
10	Bangkok	44.40	0.00	16.25	8.40	8.47	11.27
11	Dubai	33.14	13.60	10.63	4.00	2.37	2.55
12	Jakarta	32.70	4.80	13.00	5.60	7.12	2.18
13	Mumbai	32.58	11.40	10.23	5.44	4.31	1.20
14	Almaty	30.56	6.40	11.88	4.00	6.10	2.18
15	Amman	29.11	4.80	10.00	6.80	2.78	4.73
16	Riyadh	26.79	2.40	10.00	5.40	6.44	2.55
17	Quezon City	23.99	2.40	7.50	7.60	5.76	0.73
18	Colombo	21.40	2.40	10.00	5.20	3.80	0.00
19	Karachi	20.88	2.40	9.38	3.60	4.41	1.09
20	Kuwait City	19.96	2.40	6.88	3.20	7.12	0.36
21	Beirut	16.75	2.40	8.13	2.40	2.37	1.45
22	Tashkent	9.78	0.00	9.38	0.40	0.00	0.00
23	Baku	7.78	0.00	6.25	0.80	0.00	0.73

Table 3-4. *Results of Evaluation in European Cities (2009)*

Rank	City	Score	Privacy	Usability	Content	Services	Partici- pation
1	Prague	72.84	16.70	17.62	13.02	13.86	11.64
2	Madrid	55.59	11.20	14.38	13.20	13.90	2.91
3	Vienna	55.48	16.00	11.88	12.80	6.44	8.36
4	Paris	52.65	12.00	13.13	12.40	7.12	8.00
5	Bratislava	52.51	13.60	17.50	9.20	7.12	5.09
6	London	51.96	13.60	15.00	8.80	9.83	4.73
7	Zagreb	50.16	9.60	13.00	12.80	7.12	7.64
8	Ljubljana	49.39	8.00	13.13	11.60	10.85	5.82
9	Lisbon	48.82	8.80	15.00	10.80	9.49	4.73
10	Brussels	48.01	12.00	16.25	11.60	7.07	1.09
11	Vilnius	47.50	10.00	13.44	11.00	7.97	5.09
12	Helsinki	45.61	10.40	13.75	13.20	6.44	1.82
13	Dublin	45.16	12.00	12.50	9.60	10.51	0.56
14	Oslo	44.76	2.40	15.00	12.80	9.83	4.73
15	Berlin	42.90	12.80	10.63	7.60	6.78	5.09
16	Stock- holm	41.79	5.60	13.13	10.80	6.44	5.82
17	Warsaw	41.66	12.40	9.20	8.00	9.15	2.91
18	Tallinn	41.57	0.00	11.88	16.40	12.20	1.09
19	Moscow	40.10	4.80	12.50	8.80	7.46	6.55
20	Copen- hagen	37.78	3.20	15.63	8.80	5.42	4.73
21	Riga	36.88	5.60	12.50	10.40	4.75	3.64
22	Bucharest	34.65	2.40	15.63	8.00	6.44	2.18
23	Amster- dam	34.27	2.40	13.13	8.40	7.80	2.55
24	Sofia	33.13	6.80	8.75	5.80	8.14	3.64
25	Zurich	32.65	0.00	15.00	7.60	6.78	3.27
26	Istanbul	30.93	0.00	6.25	11.60	10.17	2.91
27	Belgrade	28.65	0.80	14.38	6.00	4.75	2.73
28	Rome	26.85	6.40	8.13	7.40	2.37	2.55
29	Skopje	26.56	0.00	12.44	5.10	7.22	1.80

30	Kiev	25.45	4.00	8.75	4.80	6.44	1.45
31	Minsk	25.40	2.40	10.00	6.00	3.73	3.27
32	Athens	24.84	3.20	13.75	4.40	2.03	1.45
33	Budapest	24.76	2.40	9.38	7.60	1.02	4.36
34	Chisinau	20.31	1.60	9.38	7.20	0.68	1.45
35	Sarajevo	12.26	0.00	7.50	4.40	0.00	0.36

Table 3-5. *Results of Evaluation in North American Cities (2009)*

Rank	City	Score	Privacy	Usability	Content	Services	Partici-pation
1	New York	61.10	12.80	13.44	13.80	15.42	5.64
2	Toronto	52.87	12.80	13.00	12.40	8.85	5.82
3	San Jose	25.57	2.40	8.13	6.40	6.10	2.55
4	Panama City	20.94	0.00	9.38	4.40	6.44	0.73
5	Mexico City	43.04	0.00	7.50	9.20	12.88	13.45
6	Santo Domingo	27.70	1.60	12.50	8.00	5.60	0.00
7	Guatemala City	21.56	0.00	12.80	2.56	5.64	0.56
8	San Salvador	20.52	0.00	9.15	6.40	4.22	0.75
9	San Juan	20.53	0.00	11.25	4.80	3.39	1.09

Table 3-6. *Overall Results of Evaluation in Oceanic Cities (2009)*

Rank	City	Score	Privacy	Usability	Content	Services	Partici-pation
1	Auckland	55.28	10.40	14.38	16.80	6.07	7.64
2	Sydney	41.91	12.80	12.50	9.00	5.42	2.18

Table 3-7. *Results of Evaluation in South American Cities (2009)*

Rank	City	Score	Privacy	Usability	Content	Services	Partici-pation
1	Sao Paulo	45.98	6.60	15.63	11.00	10.20	2.55
2	Buenos Aires	43.59	4.80	12.50	12.00	8.47	5.82
3	Santa Fé de Bogotá	37.85	3.20	15.00	12.80	5.40	1.45
4	Montevi-deo	35.02	0.00	13.13	11.60	8.47	1.82
5	Lima	29.76	0.00	13.75	6.40	7.80	1.82
6	Guayaquil	25.47	2.40	10.00	7.60	4.75	0.73
7	Santiago	24.08	2.40	11.25	1.60	6.10	2.73
8	Santa Cruz	19.94	1.60	11.40	5.20	1.02	0.73
9	Caracas	19.33	0.00	10.63	5.60	2.37	0.73

The average scores for each continent are presented in Figure 3-1. Oceania was once again the highest ranked continent with an average score of 48.59, and Europe, with a score of 39.54, retained the second highest rank, followed closely by Asia and North America, which switched places compared to 2007. The overall average score for all municipalities is 35.93 in 2009, an increase from 3.37 in 2007, 33.11 in 2005 and 28.49 in 2003. Ranked fifth is South America, with an overall average score of 31.23, followed by Africa, with an average score of 24.06.

Fig 3-1. *Average Score by Continent (2009)*

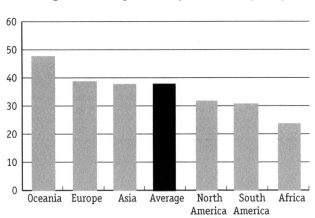

Table 3-8. *Average Score by Continent (2009)*

	Oceania	Europe	Asia	Average	North America	South America	Africa
Overall Averages	48.59	39.54	37.13	35.93	32.65	31.23	24.06

OECD Member Data

Seoul was the highest ranked OECD municipality and Hong Kong was the highest ranked non-OECD in 2007. Tables 3-9 and 3-10 present the overall score for each municipality grouped into OECD member countries and non-OECD member countries.

Table 3-9. *Results for OECD Member Countries (2009)*

Rank	City	Country	Score
1	Seoul	Republic of Korea	84.74
2	Prague	Czech Republic	72.84
3	New York	USA	61.10
4	Madrid	Spain	55.59
5	Vienna	Austria	55.48
6	Auckland	New Zealand	55.28
7	Toronto	Canada	52.87
8	Paris	France	52.65
9	Bratislava	Slovakia	52.51
10	London	UK	51.96
11	Tokyo	Japan	50.59
12	Lisbon	Portugal	48.82
13	Brussels	Belgium	48.01
14	Helsinki	Finland	45.61
15	Dublin	Ireland	45.16
16	Oslo	Norway	44.76
17	Mexico City	Mexico	43.04
18	Berlin	Germany	42.90
19	Sydney	Australia	41.91
20	Stockholm	Sweden	41.79
21	Warsaw	Poland	41.66
22	Copenhagen	Denmark	37.78

Table 3-9. *Continued*

Rank	City	Country	Score
23	Riga	Latvia	36.88
24	Amsterdam	Netherlands	34.27
25	Zurich	Switzerland	32.65
26	Rome	Italy	26.85
27	Athens	Greece	24.84
28	Budapest	Hungary	24.76

Table 3-10. *Results for OECD Non-Member Countries (2009)*

Rank	City	Country	Score
1	Hong Kong	Hong Kong	62.83
2	Singapore	Singapore	58.81
3	Shanghai	China	57.41
4	Jerusalem	Israel	50.64
5	Zagreb	Croatia	50.16
6	Ljubljana	Slovenia	49.39
7	Johannesburg	South Africa	47.68
8	Vilnius	Lithuania	47.50
9	Ho Chi Minh City	Vietnam	47.12
10	Tehran	Iran	46.17
11	Sao Paulo	Brazil	45.98
12	Kuala Lumpur	Malaysia	45.87
13	Bangkok	Thailand	44.40
14	Buenos Aires	Argentina	43.59
15	Tallinn	Estonia	41.57
16	Moscow	Russia	40.10
17	Santa Fé de Bogotá	Colombia	37.85
18	Montevideo	Uruguay	35.02
19	Bucharest	Romania	34.65
20	Dubai	UAE	33.14
21	Sofia	Bulgaria	33.13
22	Jakarta	Indonesia	32.70
23	Mumbai	India	32.58

24	Tunis	Tunisia	32.05
25	Cairo	Egypt	31.83
26	Istanbul	Turkey	30.93
27	Almaty	Kazakhstan	30.56
28	Lima	Peru	29.76
29	Amman	Jordan	29.11
30	Belgrade	Serbia	28.65
31	Santo Domingo	Dominican Republic	27.70
32	Riyadh	Saudi Arabia	26.79
33	Skopje	Macedonia	26.56
34	San Jose	Costa Rica	25.57
35	Guayaquil	Ecuador	25.47
36	Kiev	Ukraine	25.45
37	Minsk	Belarus	25.40
38	Santiago	Chile	24.08
39	Quezon City	Philippines	23.99
40	Casablanca	Morocco	22.39
41	Guatemala City	Guatemala	21.56
42	Colombo	Sri Lanka	21.40
43	Panama City	Panama	20.94
44	Lagos	Nigeria	20.94
45	Karachi	Pakistan	20.88
46	San Juan	Puerto Rico	20.53
47	San Salvador	El Salvador	20.52
48	Chisinau	Moldova	20.31
49	Kuwait City	Kuwait	19.96
50	Santa Cruz	Bolivia	19.94
51	Caracas	Venezuela	19.33
52	Lusaka	Zambia	19.02
53	Kampala	Uganda	17.69
54	Beirut	Lebanon	16.75
55	Accra	Ghana	14.28
56	Sarajevo	Bosnia and Herzegovina	12.26
57	Nairobi	Kenya	10.61
58	Tashkent	Uzbekistan	9.78
59	Baku	Azerbaijan	7.78

The results above are further analyzed (below) through grouped averages. Figure 3-2 highlights how the OECD member countries have a combined average of 46.69, well above the overall average for all municipalities, 35.93. Non-OECD member countries have an overall average of 30.83. The increase for OECD member countries from 2007 was only 1.69 points, and for non-OECD member countries there was an increase of 3.37 from 2007.

To further highlight the results between OECD and non-OECD member countries, the results presented below distinguish results by the five e-governance categories. Table 3-11 presents the scores for OECD member countries, non-OECD member countries and overall average scores for each of the e-governance categories. As would be expected, the average score for OECD member countries in each e-governance category is higher than the overall average score for each category. For non-OECD member countries, the average scores in each category are lower than the overall averages for each category.

Figure 3-2. *Average Score of Cities in OECD Member and Non-Member Countries (2009)*

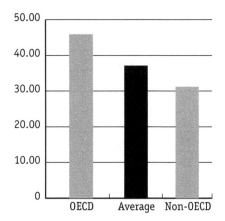

Table 3-11. *Average Score of E-governance Categories in OECD Member and Non-Member Countries (2009)*

	Privacy/ Security	Usability	Content	Service	Citizen Participation
OECD	9.23	13.39	10.72	8.31	5.03
Overall Average	5.57	11.96	8.21	6.68	3.50
Non-OECD	3.84	11.28	7.02	5.91	2.77

The overall results presented in this chapter highlight an overall increase in scores among municipalities surveyed. The results of the evaluation will be discussed in further detail in the following chapters.

Longitudinal Assessment

This chapter outlines the comparison between the findings from the 2003, 2005 and 2007 evaluations and the findings of the 2009 evaluation. The overall average score for municipalities surveyed has increased to 35.93 in 2009 from 33.37 in 2007, 33.11 in 2005 and 28.49 in 2003 (Figure 4-1). This would be the expectation for the municipalities' increasing utilization of technology to enhance effectiveness and efficiency. Table 4-1 and Figure 4-2 (see next page) highlight these increases by continent.

Figure 4-1. *Average E-Governance Score 2003–2009*

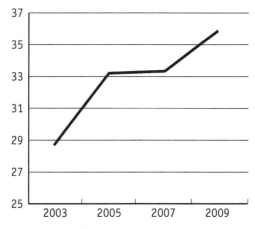

Oceania was once again the highest ranked continent, with an average score of 48.59, increasing from a score of 47.37 in 2007. Except for North America, all regions have collectively improved their e-governance performance from 2007. Europe, with a score of 39.54, retained the second highest rank, followed closely by Asia and North America, with scores of 37.13 and 32.65 respectively.

Table 4-1. *Average Score by Continent 2003–2009*

	Oceania	Europe	Asia	Average	North America	South America	Africa
2009 Overall Averages	48.59	39.54	37.13	35.93	32.65	31.23	24.06
2007 Overall Averages	47.37	37.55	33.26	33.37	33.77	28.2	16.87
2005 Overall Averages	49.94	37.17	33.05	33.11	30.21	20.45	24.87
2003 Overall Averages	46.01	30.23	30.38	28.49	27.42	20.05	17.66

Figure 4-2. *Average Score by Continent for 2003–2009*

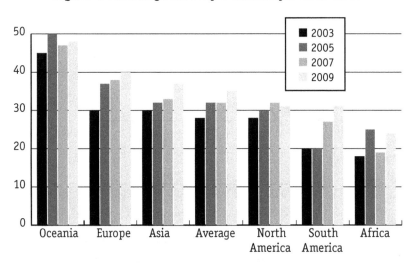

The overall average score for all municipalities is 35.93 for 2009, an increase from 33.37 in 2007, 33.11 in 2005 and 28.49 in 2003. Our survey results indicate that the number of cities with official websites has increased to 87%, compared to 86% in 2007. The improvement in scores from 2003 to 2007, represented by both OECD and non-OECD member countries, is shown in Table 4-2.

Table 4-2. *Average Scores by OECD Member and Non-Member Countries 2003–2009*

	OECD	Average	Non-OECD
2009 Overall Averages	46.69	35.93	30.83
2007 Overal Averages	45.0	33.37	27.46
2005 Overall Averages	44.35	33.11	26.50
2003 Overall Averages	36.34	28.49	24.36

Municipalities surveyed from OECD member countries increased in average score from 45 to 46.69. Municipalities surveyed from non-OECD member countries increased in average score from 27.46 to 30.83. The increase for OECD member countries from 2007 was only 1.69 points, and for non-OECD member countries it had gone up to 3.37 from 2007.

More importantly, the gap between OECD and non-OECD member countries has continued to decrease, since the 2005 evaluation. The difference between the average scores of OECD and non-OECD member countries, in 2003, was 12.08, which increased to 17.85 in the 2005 evaluation. Based on the 2007 evaluations, the gap had begun to decrease to 17.54 and finally to 15.86 in 2009. More effort is needed in non-OECD countries to bridge the digital gap and it is very important for international organizations such as the UN and cities in advanced countries to support these efforts.

Table 4-3. *Average Score by E-Governance Categories 2003–2009*

	Privacy/ Security	Usability	Content	Service	Citizen Participation
2009 Average Scores	5.57	11.96	8.21	6.68	3.50
2007 Average Scores	4.49	11.95	7.58	5.8	3.55
2005 Average Scores	4.17	12.42	7.63	5.32	3.57
2003 Average Scores	2.53	11.45	6.43	4.82	3.26

Among the five categories, Privacy/Security, Content and Services have continued to increase among municipalities across the world. It is important to note that the most significant improvement in average score is in the area of Services. The category of Usability still recorded the highest average score, while Citizen Participation continues as the category with the lowest average score. Cities are yet to recognize the importance of involving and supporting citizen participation online. A promising finding in terms of citizen participation, however, is the growing tendency in municipalities to publish performance measurement data on their websites. Specific increases in the five e-governance categories are discussed in the following chapters. Table 4-3 and Figure 4-4 highlight these findings.

Figure 4-4. *Average Score by Categories 2003–2009*

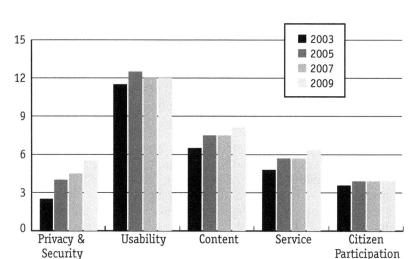

CHAPTER 5

Privacy and Security

Privacy and security results indicate, that Seoul, Prague, Vienna, Ho Chi Minh, Bratislava, London and Dubai are top ranked cities in this category. Seoul retains the first position from the 2007 survey while the other cities are new to the top five. Prague was ranked 19th in 2007 but has significantly improved to 2nd position in overall ranking with a score of 16.70 in 2009, out of a maximum score of 20. Vienna was ranked 13th in 2007 with a score of 10.40, but has also improved to 3rd overall with a score of 16.0 in 2007. Similarly Ho Chi Minh has improved from 24th rank with a score of 8.4 to 4th position overall with a score of 14.40. Table 5-1 summarizes the results for all the municipalities evaluated in this category.

The average score in this category is 5.57, an increase from a score of 4.49 in 2007. Eighteen cities evaluated earned 0 points in this category, a decrease in the total number of municipalities that earned 0 points in 2007 (26), 2005 (31) and 2003 (36). Many cities still have not properly understood the importance of a privacy and security policy, a vital deficiency in the process of development of digital governance.

Table 5-1. *Results in Privacy and Security (2009)*

Rank	City	Country	Privacy
1	Seoul	Republic of Korea	18.80
2	Prague	Czech Republic	16.70
3	Vienna	Austria	16.00
4	Ho Chi Minh City	Vietnam	14.40
5	Bratislava	Slovakia	13.60
5	London	UK	13.60
5	Dubai	UAE	13.60
8	New York	USA	12.80
8	Toronto	Canada	12.80
8	Berlin	Germany	12.80
8	Sydney	Australia	12.80
12	Tehran	Iran	12.56

Table 5-1. *Continued*

Rank	City	Country	Privacy
13	Warsaw	Poland	12.40
14	Paris	France	12.00
14	Brussels	Belgium	12.00
14	Dublin	Ireland	12.00
17	Mumbai	India	11.40
18	Hong Kong	Hong Kong	11.20
18	Shanghai	China	11.20
18	Madrid	Spain	11.20
21	Auckland	New Zealand	10.40
21	Kuala Lumpur	Malaysia	10.40
21	Helsinki	Finland	10.40
24	Vilnius	Lithuania	10.00
25	Zagreb	Croatia	9.60
26	Jerusalem	Israel	8.80
26	Lisbon	Portugal	8.80
28	Tokyo	Japan	8.00
28	Ljubljana	Slovenia	8.00
30	Sofia	Bulgaria	6.80
31	Sao Paulo	Brazil	6.60
32	Singapore	Singapore	6.40
32	Almaty	Kazakhstan	6.40
32	Rome	Italy	6.40
35	Stockholm	Sweden	5.60
35	Riga	Latvia	5.60
37	Buenos Aires	Argentina	4.80
37	Moscow	Russia	4.80
37	Jakarta	Indonesia	4.80
37	Amman	Jordan	4.80
37	Lagos	Nigeria	4.80
42	Johannesburg	South Africa	4.00
42	Kiev	Ukraine	4.00
44	Santa Fé de Bogotá	Colombia	3.20

44	Copenhagen	Denmark	3.20
44	Athens	Greece	3.20
47	Oslo	Norway	2.40
47	Bucharest	Romania	2.40
47	Amsterdam	Netherlands	2.40
47	Cairo	Egypt	2.40
47	Riyadh	Saudi Arabia	2.40
47	San Jose	Costa Rica	2.40
47	Guayaquil	Ecuador	2.40
47	Minsk	Belarus	2.40
47	Budapest	Hungary	2.40
47	Santiago	Chile	2.40
47	Quezon City	Philippines	2.40
47	Casablanca	Morocco	2.40
47	Colombo	Sri Lanka	2.40
47	Karachi	Pakistan	2.40
47	Kuwait City	Kuwait	2.40
47	Lusaka	Zambia	2.40
47	Kampala	Uganda	2.40
47	Beirut	Lebanon	2.40
47	Nairobi	Kenya	2.40
66	Santo Domingo	Dominican Republic	1.60
66	Chisinau	Moldova	1.60
66	Santa Cruz	Bolivia	1.60
69	Belgrade	Serbia	0.80
70	Bangkok	Thailand	0.00
70	Mexico City	Mexico	0.00
70	Tallinn	Estonia	0.00
70	Montevideo	Uruguay	0.00
70	Zurich	Switzerland	0.00
70	Tunis	Tunisia	0.00
70	Istanbul	Turkey	0.00
70	Lima	Peru	0.00
70	Skopje	Macedonia	0.00
70	Guatemala City	Guatemala	0.00

Table 5-1. *Continued*

Rank	City	Country	Privacy
70	Panama City	Panama	0.00
70	San Juan	Puerto Rico	0.00
70	San Salvador	El Salvador	0.00
70	Caracas	Venezuela	0.00
70	Accra	Ghana	0.00
70	Sarajevo	Bosnia and Herzegovina	0.00
70	Tashkent	Uzbekistan	0.00
70	Baku	Azerbaijan	0.00

Table 5-2 represents the average score in Privacy and Security by continent. Oceania remained as the continent with the highest average scores with 11.60 points, which increased from 9.20 in 2007. Africa replaced South America as the continent with the lowest average score. Cities in OECD countries scored an average of 9.23, while cities in non-member countries scored only 3.84 in this category. These results indicate that cities in economically advanced countries continue to have more emphasis on privacy and security policy than do cities in less developed countries. Figures 5-1 and 5-2 illustrate the data presented in Table 5-2.

Figure 5-1. *Average Score in Privacy and Security by Continent (2009)*

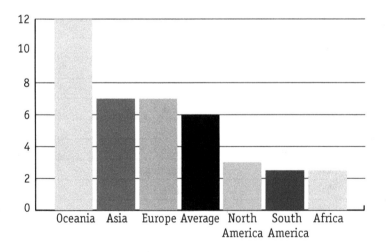

Table 5-2. *Average Score in Privacy and Security by Continent (2009)*

	Oceania	Asia	Europe	Average	North America	South America	Africa
Privacy Averages	11.60	6.83	6.66	5.57	3.29	2.33	2.31

Figure 5-2. *Average Score in Privacy and Security by OECD Member and Non-Member Countries (2009)*

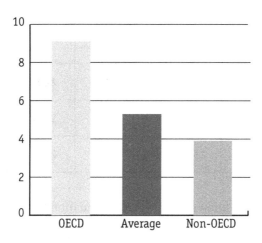

Table 5-3 lists the results of evaluation of key aspects in the category of Privacy and Security, by continent. Overall, cities across the world are found to pay more attention to privacy and security matters on their websites, based on the comparison between the 2009 and 2007 surveys. All cities evaluated in Oceania, 66% of cities in Europe, 61% of cities in Asia, and 56% of cities in North America have developed a privacy or security statement/policy. However, only 33% of cities in South America and 11% of the cities in Africa have developed privacy statements for their websites. The overall percentage for cities that have a privacy or security policy online is 55%, a significant increase from 47% in 2007, 37% in 2005 and 22.5% in 2003.

With regard to the use of encryption in the transmission of data, all of the cities evaluated in Oceania, as well as 63% of the cities in Europe, 39% in Asia, and 22% of the cities in North America have a policy addressing the use of encryption on their websites. The overall percentage for cities that have a policy addressing the use of encryption online is 39%, a significant increase from 26% in 2007, 21% in 2005 and 5% in 2003. In addition, all cities evaluated in Oceania, 51% of cities in Europe, and 35% of cities in Asia have a policy addressing the use of "cookies" or "web beacons" to track users. The overall percentage for cities that have a policy addressing the use of "cookies" or "web beacons" to track users is 36%, also an increase of 27% in 2007, from 23% in 2005 and 5% in 2003.

Table 5-3. *Results for Privacy and Security by Continent (2009)*

	Oceania	Europe	Asia	Average	North America	South America	Africa
Privacy or Security Policy	100%	66%	61%	55%	56%	33%	11%
Use of encryption	100%	63%	39%	39%	22%	11%	0%
Use of cookies	100%	51%	35%	36%	33%	11%	0%
Digital Signature	100%	23%	9%	17%	22%	11%	0%

There were no cities worldwide in the 2003 evaluation that had a privacy policy addressing the use of digital signatures to authenticate users. However, 9% of municipalities in the 2005 evaluation did address the use of digital signatures. This percentage increased to 17% in the 2009 evaluation.

Table 5-4 lists the results of evaluation of key aspects in the category of Privacy and Security by OECD and non-OECD member countries. Overall, cities in OECD countries continue to pay more attention to privacy and security matters on their websites than cities in non-OECD countries. About 82% of cities evaluated in OECD countries have developed a privacy or security statement/ policy, while about 42% of cities in non-OECD countries have a privacy statement on their websites. With regard to the use of encryption in the transmission of data, some 46% of cities evaluated in OECD countries have a privacy policy addressing the use of encryption, compared to 36% of cities in non-OECD countries. In addition, 68% of cities evaluated in OECD countries have a privacy policy addressing the use of "cookies" or "web beacons" to track users, while only 22% of cities in non-OECD countries have statements as to the use of "cookies." Overall, cities in OECD countries score above average throughout the world.

Table 5-4. *Results for Privacy and Security by OECD Member and Non-Member Countries (2009)*

	OECD	Average	Non-OECD
Privacy or Security Policy	82%	55%	42%
Use of encryption	46%	39%	36%
Use of cookies	68%	36%	22%
Digital Signature	34%	17%	14%

In terms of queries, whether the site has a privacy or security statement/policy, in 2009 about 55% of cities had privacy and security policies compared to 47% in 2007. More than half of the cities, however, have not yet provided citizens with a privacy and security statement (Figure 5-3). Seoul, Prague, Vienna, Ho Chi Minh and Bratislava have clear privacy or security statements/ policies, as reflected by their rankings in the category.

Figure 5-3. *Existence of Privacy or Security Statement/Policy (2009)*

■ Privacy/Security
No Privacy/Security Statement

CHAPTER 6

Usability

The following chapter highlights the results for Usability. Results indicate that Prague, Seoul, Bratislava, Singapore and Cairo are top ranked cities in the category of Usability. Except Seoul, the other cities are new to the top five rankings. Prague ranks first with a score of 17.62 out of a maximum score of 20, followed by Seoul and Bratislava in second place with a score of 17.50. Singapore and Cairo are ranked 4th with a score of 16.88. Table 6-1 summarizes the results for all the municipalities evaluated in the category.

The average score in this category is 11.96, an increase from a score of 11.95 in 2007. Cities in OECD countries scored an average of 13.39, while cities in non-member countries scored only 11.28 in this category. Overall, cities in Oceania scored the highest average of 13.44, while cities in Africa scored the lowest average of 10.35 in the category of Usability.

Table 6-1. *Results in Usability (2009)*

Rank	City	Country	Usability
1	Prague	Czech Republic	17.62
2	Seoul	Republic of Korea	17.50
2	Bratislava	Slovakia	17.50
4	Singapore	Singapore	16.88
4	Cairo	Egypt	16.88
6	Brussels	Belgium	16.25
6	Johannesburg	South Africa	16.25
6	Bangkok	Thailand	16.25
9	Jerusalem	Israel	15.63
9	Sao Paulo	Brazil	15.63
9	Copenhagen	Denmark	15.63
9	Bucharest	Romania	15.63
13	Hong Kong	Hong Kong	15.31
14	London	UK	15.00

Table 6-1. *Continued*

Rank	City	Country	Usability
14	Lisbon	Portugal	15.00
14	Ho Chi Minh City	Vietnam	15.00
14	Oslo	Norway	15.00
14	Santa Fé de Bogotá	Colombia	15.00
14	Zurich	Switzerland	15.00
14	Tunis	Tunisia	15.00
21	Madrid	Spain	14.38
21	Auckland	New Zealand	14.38
21	Belgrade	Serbia	14.38
24	Tokyo	Japan	14.25
25	Tehran	Iran	13.75
25	Helsinki	Finland	13.75
25	Lima	Peru	13.75
25	Athens	Greece	13.75
29	New York	USA	13.44
29	Vilnius	Lithuania	13.44
31	Paris	France	13.13
31	Ljubljana	Slovenia	13.13
31	Stockholm	Sweden	13.13
31	Montevideo	Uruguay	13.13
31	Amsterdam	Netherlands	13.13
36	Toronto	Canada	13.00
36	Zagreb	Croatia	13.00
36	Jakarta	Indonesia	13.00
39	Guatemala City	Guatemala	12.80
40	Dublin	Ireland	12.50
40	Buenos Aires	Argentina	12.50
40	Sydney	Australia	12.50
40	Moscow	Russia	12.50
40	Riga	Latvia	12.50
40	Santo Domingo	Dominican Republic	12.50
46	Skopje	Macedonia	12.44
47	Vienna	Austria	11.88
47	Kuala Lumpur	Malaysia	11.88

47	Tallinn	Estonia	11.88
47	Almaty	Kazakhstan	11.88
51	Santa Cruz	Bolivia	11.40
52	Shanghai	China	11.25
52	Santiago	Chile	11.25
52	Casablanca	Morocco	11.25
52	San Juan	Puerto Rico	11.25
56	Berlin	Germany	10.63
56	Dubai	UAE	10.63
56	Caracas	Venezuela	10.63
59	Mumbai	India	10.23
60	Amman	Jordan	10.00
60	Riyadh	Saudi Arabia	10.00
60	Guayaquil	Ecuador	10.00
60	Minsk	Belarus	10.00
60	Colombo	Sri Lanka	10.00
60	Kampala	Uganda	10.00
66	Karachi	Pakistan	9.38
66	Budapest	Hungary	9.38
66	Panama City	Panama	9.38
66	Chisinau	Moldova	9.38
66	Tashkent	Uzbekistan	9.38
71	Warsaw	Poland	9.20
72	San Salvador	El Salvador	9.15
73	Sofia	Bulgaria	8.75
73	Kiev	Ukraine	8.75
75	Rome	Italy	8.13
75	San Jose	Costa Rica	8.13
75	Beirut	Lebanon	8.13
78	Mexico City	Mexico	7.50
78	Quezon City	Philippines	7.50
78	Sarajevo	Bosnia and Herzegovina	7.50
81	Kuwait City	Kuwait	6.88
82	Istanbul	Turkey	6.25
82	Lusaka	Zambia	6.25
82	Accra	Ghana	6.25

Table 6-1. *Continued*

Rank	City	Country	Content
82	Nairobi	Kenya	6.25
82	Baku	Azerbaijan	6.25
87	Lagos	Nigeria	5.00

Table 6-2 represents the average score in Usability. Overall, cities in Oceania scored the highest average of 13.44, while cities in Africa scored the lowest average of 10.35 in this category. South America ranks second with a score of 12.59 and Europe follows closely in the third position with a score of 12.56. Table 6-2 also presents the data separated by OECD and Non-OECD member countries for the category of Usability. Cities in OECD countries scored an average of 13.39, while cities in non-member countries scored only 11.28 in this category. This result indicates that cities in economically advanced countries continue to have more emphasis on usability than do cities in less developed countries; however, the gap has slightly decreased from that in 2007. Figures 6-1 and 6-2 illustrate the data presented in Table 6-2.

Table 6-2. *Average Score in Usability by Continent and OECD Member and Non-Member Countries (2009)*

	Oceania	South America	Europe	Average	Asia	North America	Africa
Usability Averages	13.44	12.59	12.56	11.96	11.78	10.79	10.35

Figure 6-1. *Average Score in Usability by Continent (2009)*

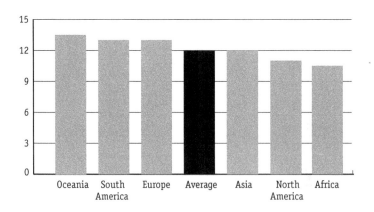

Table 6-3 lists the results of the evaluation of key aspects in the category of Usability by continent. In terms of homepage length, with text size set to "medium" at the "view" menu of Internet Explorer on a 17 inch monitor, cities in Europe, North America, South America, Asia, and Oceania score above average, while cities in Africa are below average. That is, under the conditions above, many cities in Europe, North America, South America, Asia and Oceania require two screens or less to view the main city homepage.

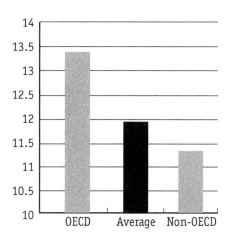

Figure 6-2. *Average Score in Usability by OECD Member and Non-Member Countries (2009)*

With respect to targeted audience links, 71% of cities in Europe, 67% of cities in South America and 78% in Africa have the targeted audience links divided into more than three categories (e.g. general citizens, youth, the elderly, women, family, citizens in need of social welfare services, businesses, industry, small businesses, public employees, etc.), while on average 70% of all cities have such links. Also, as to a site map, 77% in Europe and 67% in South America have a sitemap containing active links and less than two screens in length, whereas 100% cities in Oceania and 74% of cities in Africa provide sitemaps online. Moreover, in terms of online search tools, all cities in Oceania, about 89% of cities in Europe and 81% in Asia are found to provide online search tools.

Table 6-3. *Results for Usability by Continent (2009)*

	Europe	South America	Africa	Average	Asia	Oceania	North America
Targeted Audience	71%	67%	78%	70%	70%	50%	67%
Site map	77%	67%	67%	72%	74%	100%	56%
Search tool	94%	89%	44%	86%	81%	100%	78%

Table 6-4 indicates the results of assessments of usability among OECD and non-OECD countries. In terms of targeted audience links, about 82% of cities in OECD countries have links divided into more than three categories, while only 64% of non-OECD countries have such links. As to site maps, about 72% of cities throughout the world have a sitemap containing active links and less than two screens in length. Also, about 96% of cities in OECD countries and 81% in non-OECD countries provide online search tools.

Table 6-4. *Results for Usability by OECD Member and Non-Member Countries (2009)*

	OECD	Average	Non-OECD
Targeted Audience	82%	70%	64%
Site map	82%	72%	69%
Search tool	96%	86%	81%

With regard to "Targeted audience links: Are targeted audience links available on the homepage?" (e.g. general citizens, youth, the elderly, women, citizens in need of social welfare services, businesses, industry, public employees, etc.)," 63% of municipal websites are divided into more than three categories, (Figure 6-3).

Figure 6-3. *Targeted Audience Links (2009)*

■ Three Catagories or More

▨ Two Catagories or Less

CHAPTER 7

Content

Results for Content indicate that Seoul, Auckland, Tallinn, Hong Kong and New York are top ranked cities in this category. New to the top five are Auckland, Tallinn and New York. Auckland was ranked 30th in 2007 with a score of 8.60, but has improved to second overall with a score of 16.80 in 2009, out of a maximum score of 20. Tallinn was also ranked 30th in 2007, but has improved to third overall with a score of 16.40 in 2009. New York was ranked 9th in 2007 with a score of 13.20, but is now ranked fifth with a score of 13.80. Table 7-1 summarizes the results for all the municipalities evaluated in the Content category.

The average score for the top five ranked cities in 2009 is 15.92, while the average score for the top five ranked cities was 16.16 in 2007 and 14.33 in 2005. However the overall average score for this category has increased from 7.63 in 2007 to a score of 8.21 in 2009.

Table 7-1. *Results in Content (2009)*

Rank	City	Country	Content
1	Seoul	Republic of Korea	18.20
2	Auckland	New Zealand	16.80
3	Tallinn	Estonia	16.40
4	Hong Kong	Hong Kong	14.40
5	New York	USA	13.80
6	Jerusalem	Israel	13.60
7	Madrid	Spain	13.20
7	Helsinki	Finland	13.20
9	Prague	Czech Republic	13.02
10	Vienna	Austria	12.80
10	Zagreb	Croatia	12.80
10	Oslo	Norway	12.80
10	Santa Fé de Bogotá	Colombia	12.80

Table 7-1. *Continued*

Rank	City	Country	Content
14	Toronto	Canada	12.40
14	Paris	France	12.40
14	Tokyo	Japan	12.40
17	Buenos Aires	Argentina	12.00
18	Ljubljana	Slovenia	11.60
18	Brussels	Belgium	11.60
18	Montevideo	Uruguay	11.60
18	Istanbul	Turkey	11.60
22	Vilnius	Lithuania	11.00
22	Sao Paulo	Brazil	11.00
24	Lisbon	Portugal	10.80
24	Stockholm	Sweden	10.80
26	Riga	Latvia	10.40
27	Shanghai	China	10.00
28	Singapore	Singapore	9.60
28	Dublin	Ireland	9.60
30	Kuala Lumpur	Malaysia	9.40
31	Bratislava	Slovakia	9.20
31	Ho Chi Minh City	Vietnam	9.20
31	Mexico City	Mexico	9.20
34	Sydney	Australia	9.00
35	London	UK	8.80
35	Johannesburg	South Africa	8.80
35	Moscow	Russia	8.80
35	Copenhagen	Denmark	8.80
39	Bangkok	Thailand	8.40
39	Amsterdam	Netherlands	8.40
39	Lagos	Nigeria	8.40
42	Tehran	Iran	8.20
43	Warsaw	Poland	8.00
43	Bucharest	Romania	8.00
43	Cairo	Egypt	8.00
43	Santo Domingo	Dominican Republic	8.00

47	Berlin	Germany	7.60
47	Zurich	Switzerland	7.60
47	Tunis	Tunisia	7.60
47	Guayaquil	Ecuador	7.60
47	Budapest	Hungary	7.60
47	Quezon City	Philippines	7.60
53	Rome	Italy	7.40
54	Chisinau	Moldova	7.20
55	Amman	Jordan	6.80
56	Lima	Peru	6.40
56	San Jose	Costa Rica	6.40
56	San Salvador	El Salvador	6.40
59	Belgrade	Serbia	6.00
59	Minsk	Belarus	6.00
61	Sofia	Bulgaria	5.80
62	Jakarta	Indonesia	5.60
62	Casablanca	Morocco	5.60
62	Caracas	Venezuela	5.60
65	Mumbai	India	5.44
66	Riyadh	Saudi Arabia	5.40
67	Colombo	Sri Lanka	5.20
67	Santa Cruz	Bolivia	5.20
69	Skopje	Macedonia	5.10
70	Kiev	Ukraine	4.80
70	San Juan	Puerto Rico	4.80
70	Lusaka	Zambia	4.80
73	Athens	Greece	4.40
73	Panama City	Panama	4.40
73	Sarajevo	Bosnia and Herzegovina	4.40
76	Dubai	UAE	4.00
76	Almaty	Kazakhstan	4.00
78	Karachi	Pakistan	3.60
78	Kampala	Uganda	3.60
80	Kuwait City	Kuwait	3.20
81	Accra	Ghana	2.80

Table 7-1. *Continued*

Rank	City	Country	Content
82	Guatemala City	Guatemala	2.56
83	Beirut	Lebanon	2.40
84	Santiago	Chile	1.60
84	Nairobi	Kenya	1.60
86	Baku	Azerbaijan	0.80
87	Tashkent	Uzbekistan	0.40

Table 7-2 represents the average score in Content by continent. Overall, cities in Europe scored 9.37, while cities in Africa scored only 5.69 in this category. Oceania replaced Europe as the continent with the highest average score with a rating of 12.90 in 2009. Africa remained the continent with the lowest average score of 5.69, which increased from 4.33 in 2007. Table 7-2 also presents the data separated by OECD and non-OECD member countries for the category of Content. Cities in OECD countries scored an average of 10.72, while cities in non-member countries scored only 7.02 in this category. Cities in economically advanced countries continue to have more emphasis on website content than do cities in less developed countries. Figures 7-1 and 7-2 illustrate the data presented in Table 7-2.

Table 7-2. *Average Score in Content by Continent and OECD Member and Non-Member Countries (2009)*

	Oceania	Europe	Average	South America	North America	Asia	Africa
Content Averages	12.90	9.37	8.21	8.20	7.55	7.30	5.69

Table 7-3 indicates the results of evaluation of Content by continent. More than 30% of cities evaluated in all continents, except the Americas, have websites with mechanisms in the area of emergency management or alert mechanisms (severe weather, etc.). Also, with regard to disability access for the blind, only about 17% of cites have websites providing such access (e.g. Bobby compliant: http://www.cast.org/bobby). European cities continue to have the highest percentage of municipal websites with that feature. In addition, about 21% of cities have websites providing disability access for the deaf (TDD phone service). Cities in Oceania and Africa have no websites providing disability access for the blind.

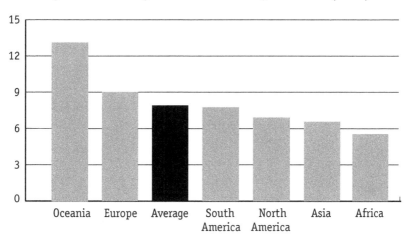

Figure 7-1. *Average Score in Content by Continent (2009)*

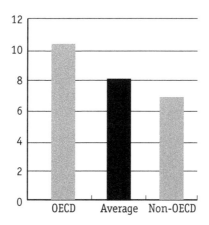

Figure 7-2. *Average Score in Content by OECD Member and Non-Member Countries (2009)*

With respect to the use of wireless technology, 37% of cities in Europe and 33% in North America have websites using wireless technology, such as messages to a mobile phone or PDA (Personal Digital Assistant) to update applications, events etc. No cities in Oceania and Africa have websites using this technology. Also, more than half of cities in Asia, and Europe have websites offering access in more than one language.

Table 7-3. *Results for Content by Continent (2009)*

	Oceania	Europe	Average	Asia	North America	South America	Africa
Emergency Management	50%	34%	39%	61%	22%	22%	33%
Access for the Blind	0%	31%	17%	17%	11%	11%	0%
Access for the deaf	50%	20%	21%	22%	22%	22%	11%
Wireless technology	0%	37%	31%	30%	33%	11%	0%
More than one language	50%	77%	59%	70%	22%	22%	33%

Table 7-4 indicates the results of assessments of Content among OECD and non-OECD countries. Like the other categories discussed above, cities in OECD countries have more advanced websites in terms of content than do cities in non-OECD countries. As to an emergency management or an alert mechanism, 61% of cities in OECD countries have such websites, with only 26% of cities in non-OECD member countries having such capacities.

With regard to disability access for the blind, about 36% of cites in OECD countries have websites providing such access, whereas only 8% of cities in non-OECD countries have that capacity. In addition, about 32% of cities in OECD countries have websites providing disability access for the deaf, while only 15% of cities in non-OECD countries offer it. With respect to the use of wireless technology, about 57% of cities in OECD countries have websites using wireless technology to update applications, events, etc. while only 14% of cities in non-OECD countries have websites using that technology. In addition, about 82% of cities in OECD countries have websites offering access in more than one language, while 47% in non-OECD countries offer multilingual access.

Table 7-4. *Results for Content by OECD Member and Non-Member Countries (2009)*

	OECD	Average	Non-OECD
Emergency Management	61%	39%	26%
Access for the blind	36%	17%	8%
Access for the deaf	32%	21%	15%
Use of wireless technology	57%	31%	14%
More than one language	82%	59%	47%

Furthermore, with respect to the question "Does the site offer access in more than one language?," 59% cities of those evaluated have a website that offers access in more than one language, while about 41% of cities have access in only one language. Figure 7-3 represents these findings in terms of overall percentages.

Figure 7-3. *Access in Multiple Languages (2009)*

■ Access in more than one language

Access in only one language

CHAPTER 8

Services

The following chapter highlights the results for online Services. Results indicate that Seoul, Singapore, New York, Shanghai and Madrid are the top ranked cities in the category of online Services. New to the top five are New York and Shanghai. Seoul ranks first with a score of 19.15 out of a maximum score of 20, followed by Singapore in second place with a score of 15.93. New York is ranked third with a score of 15.42, followed by Shanghai and Madrid with scores of 14.41 and 13.90 respectively. Table 8-1 summarizes the results for all the municipalities evaluated in this category.

The average score in this category is 6.68, an increase from a score of 5.8 in 2007, 5.32 in 2005 and 4.82 in 2003. No cities evaluated earned 0 points in this category compared to two in 2005 and three in 2003. However the average score for the top five ranked cities in 2009 is 15.76, which decreased from 16.17 in 2007. The average scores for the top five ranked cities in 2005 and 2003 were 14.51 and 13.69 respectively.

Table 8-1. *Results in Services (2009)*

Rank	City	Country	Services
1	Seoul	Republic of Korea	19.15
2	Singapore	Singapore	15.93
3	New York	USA	15.42
4	Shanghai	China	14.41
5	Madrid	Spain	13.90
6	Prague	Czech Republic	13.86
7	Hong Kong	Hong Kong	13.56
8	Mexico City	Mexico	12.88
9	Tallinn	Estonia	12.20
10	Jerusalem	Israel	11.53
11	Tokyo	Japan	10.85
11	Ljubljana	Slovenia	10.85

Table 8-1. *Continued*

Rank	City	Country	Services
13	Dublin	Ireland	10.51
14	Sao Paulo	Brazil	10.20
15	Istanbul	Turkey	10.17
16	London	UK	9.83
16	Oslo	Norway	9.83
18	Lisbon	Portugal	9.49
19	Kuala Lumpur	Malaysia	9.46
20	Warsaw	Poland	9.15
21	Toronto	Canada	8.85
22	Johannesburg	South Africa	8.81
23	Bangkok	Thailand	8.47
23	Montevideo	Uruguay	8.47
23	Buenos Aires	Argentina	8.47
26	Sofia	Bulgaria	8.14
27	Vilnius	Lithuania	7.97
28	Ho Chi Minh City	Vietnam	7.80
28	Amsterdam	Netherlands	7.80
28	Lima	Peru	7.80
31	Moscow	Russia	7.46
31	Tehran	Iran	7.46
33	Skopje	Macedonia	7.22
34	Paris	France	7.12
34	Bratislava	Slovakia	7.12
34	Zagreb	Croatia	7.12
34	Jakarta	Indonesia	7.12
34	Kuwait City	Kuwait	7.12
39	Brussels	Belgium	7.07
40	Berlin	Germany	6.78
40	Zurich	Switzerland	6.78
42	Vienna	Austria	6.44
42	Helsinki	Finland	6.44
42	Stockholm	Sweden	6.44
42	Bucharest	Romania	6.44

42	Riyadh	Saudi Arabia	6.44
42	Kiev	Ukraine	6.44
42	Panama City	Panama	6.44
49	Almaty	Kazakhstan	6.10
49	San Jose	Costa Rica	6.10
49	Santiago	Chile	6.10
52	Auckland	New Zealand	6.07
53	Quezon City	Philippines	5.76
54	Guatemala City	Guatemala	5.64
55	Santo Domingo	Dominican Republic	5.60
56	Sydney	Australia	5.42
56	Copenhagen	Denmark	5.42
58	Santa Fé de Bogotá	Colombia	5.40
59	Tunis	Tunisia	5.08
60	Riga	Latvia	4.75
60	Guayaquil	Ecuador	4.75
60	Belgrade	Serbia	4.75
63	Karachi	Pakistan	4.41
64	Mumbai	India	4.31
65	San Salvador	El Salvador	4.22
66	Colombo	Sri Lanka	3.80
67	Minsk	Belarus	3.73
68	San Juan	Puerto Rico	3.39
68	Lusaka	Zambia	3.39
70	Accra	Ghana	3.05
71	Amman	Jordan	2.78
72	Cairo	Egypt	2.37
72	Rome	Italy	2.37
72	Lagos	Nigeria	2.37
72	Caracas	Venezuela	2.37
72	Beirut	Lebanon	2.37
72	Dubai	UAE	2.37
78	Athens	Greece	2.03
79	Casablanca	Morocco	1.69
79	Kampala	Uganda	1.69

Table 8-1. *Continued*

Rank	City	Country	Services
81	Budapest	Hungary	1.02
81	Santa Cruz	Bolivia	1.02
83	Chisinau	Moldova	0.68
84	Sarajevo	Bosnia and Herzegovina	0.00
84	Nairobi	Kenya	0.00
84	Tashkent	Uzbekistan	0.00
84	Baku	Azerbaijan	0.00

Table 8-2 represents the average score of online Services by continent. Overall, cities in North America ranked highest with a score of 7.62, followed closely by Asian cities with a score of 7.44. European cities ranked third with a score of 7.07, while cities in South America ranked fourth with a score of 6.06. Table 8-2 also presents the data separated by OECD and Non-OECD member countries for the category of online Services. Cities in OECD countries scored an average of 8.31 in 2009, while cities in non-member countries recorded an average of 5.91 in this category. This result indicates that cities in developed countries have provided citizens with more online services than cities in less developed countries. Figures 8-1 and 8-2 illustrate the data in Table 8-2.

Table 8-3 indicates the results of key aspects selected in the category of Service delivery by continent. With regard to searchable databases, more than 50% of cities in Oceania, Europe and Asia have websites offering a searchable database, while less than 25% of cities evaluated in North America have sites offering that capacity. In terms of portal customization, all cities in Oceania, 17% of cities in Europe and about 26% in Asia allow users to customize the main city homepage, depending on their needs. In addition, with respect to access to private information online (e.g. educational records, medical records, point total of driving violations, lost pet dogs, lost property), all cities in Oceania and 37% of cities in Europe allow users to access private information online.Table 8-2. Average Score in Services by Continent and OECD Member and Non-Member Countries (2009)

Table 8-2. *Average Score in Services by Continent and OECD Member and Non-Member Countries (2009)*

	North America	Asia	Europe	Average	South America	Oceania	Africa
Services Averages	7.62	7.44	7.07	6.68	6.06	5.75	3.16

Figure 8-1. *Average Score in Services by Continent (2009)*

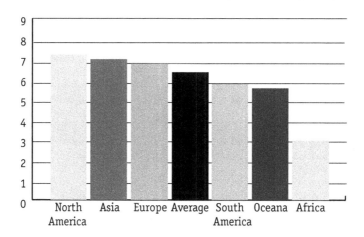

Figure 8-2. *Average Score in Services by OECD Member and* Non-Member Countries (2009)

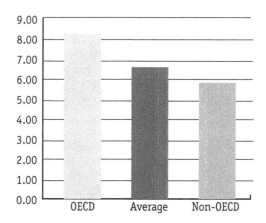

Table 8-4 (see next page) represents the results of key aspects selected in the category of service delivery by OECD membership. With regard to searchable databases, about 82% of cities in OECD countries have websites offering a searchable database, and about 49% in non-OECD countries have sites offering that capacity. In terms of portal customization, about 29% of cities in OECD countries allow users to customize the main city homepage depending on their needs, and about 14% in non-OECD countries allow citizens to do so. In addition, with respect to access to private information online, 39% of cities in OECD countries allow users to access such information, while 17% of cities in non-OECD countries allow citizens to do so.

Table 8-3. *Results for Services by Continent (2009)*

	Oceania	Europe	Asia	Average	North America	South America	Africa
Searchable Database	100%	80%	57%	59%	22%	44%	33%
Portal Customization	100%	17%	26%	18%	11%	0%	12.5%
Access to Private Info	100%	37%	17%	24%	11%	11%	0%

Table 8-4. *Results for Services by OECD Member and Non-Member Countries (2009)*

	OECD	Average	Non-OECD
Searchable Database	82%	59%	49%
Portal Customization	29%	18%	14%
Access Private Info	39%	24%	17%

Overall, 24% of all cities allow access to private information online in response to the question "Does the site allow access to private information online (e.g. educational records, medical records, point total of driving violations, lost pet dogs, lost property)?" Over 70% of cities do not allow such access. Figure 8-3 illustrates this finding.

Figure 8-3. *Access to Private Information Online (2009)*

■ Access to Private Information

　No Access to Private Information

CHAPTER 9

Citizen Participation

The following chapter highlights the results for Citizen Participation. Results indicate that Mexico City, Prague, Bangkok, Seoul and Shanghai are top ranked cities in the category of Citizen Participation. New to the top five are Mexico City, Prague, and Shanghai, among which Mexico City ranks first with a score of 13.45, out of a maximum score of 20. This is a significant improvement from its 42nd position in 2007. Prague was ranked 36th in 2007 with a score of 3.46, but has improved to second overall with a score of 11.64 in 2009. Bangkok retained the third overall ranking with a score of 11.27 in 2009. Seoul ranked fourth overall with a score of 11.09 in 2009, while Shanghai, which was ranked 38th in 2007 with a score of 3.28, has received a fifth overall ranking with a score of 10.55 in 2009. Table 9-1 summarizes the results for all the municipalities evaluated in this category.

The average score in this category is 3.50, a slight decrease from a score of 3.55 in 2007. This can be attributed to the lack of support for such online citizen participation practices among municipalities across the world.

Table 9-1. *Results in Citizen Participation (2009)*

Rank	City	Country	Participation
1	Mexico City	Mexico	13.45
2	Prague	Czech Republic	11.64
3	Bangkok	Thailand	11.27
4	Seoul	Republic of Korea	11.09
5	Shanghai	China	10.55
6	Singapore	Singapore	10.00
7	Johannesburg	South Africa	9.82
8	Vienna	Austria	8.36
8	Hong Kong	Hong Kong	8.36
10	Paris	France	8.00
11	Auckland	New Zealand	7.64

Table 9-1. *Continued*

Rank	City	Country	Participation
11	Zagreb	Croatia	7.64
13	Moscow	Russia	6.55
14	Buenos Aires	Argentina	5.82
14	Stockholm	Sweden	5.82
14	Toronto	Canada	5.82
14	Ljubljana	Slovenia	5.82
18	New York	USA	5.64
19	Bratislava	Slovakia	5.09
19	Berlin	Germany	5.09
19	Tokyo	Japan	5.09
19	Vilnius	Lithuania	5.09
23	London	UK	4.73
23	Lisbon	Portugal	4.73
23	Kuala Lumpur	Malaysia	4.73
23	Oslo	Norway	4.73
23	Copenhagen	Denmark	4.73
23	Amman	Jordan	4.73
29	Tunis	Tunisia	4.36
29	Budapest	Hungary	4.36
31	Tehran	Iran	4.20
32	Riga	Latvia	3.64
32	Sofia	Bulgaria	3.64
34	Zurich	Switzerland	3.27
34	Minsk	Belarus	3.27
36	Madrid	Spain	2.91
36	Warsaw	Poland	2.91
36	Istanbul	Turkey	2.91
39	Santiago	Chile	2.73
39	Belgrade	Serbia	2.73
41	Sao Paulo	Brazil	2.55
41	Rome	Italy	2.55
41	Amsterdam	Netherlands	2.55
41	Dubai	UAE	2.55

41	Riyadh	Saudi Arabia	2.55
41	San Jose	Costa Rica	2.55
47	Sydney	Australia	2.18
47	Bucharest	Romania	2.18
47	Cairo	Egypt	2.18
47	Almaty	Kazakhstan	2.18
47	Lusaka	Zambia	2.18
47	Accra	Ghana	2.18
47	Jakarta	Indonesia	2.18
54	Helsinki	Finland	1.82
54	Montevideo	Uruguay	1.82
54	Lima	Peru	1.82
57	Skopje	Macedonia	1.80
58	Santa Fé de Bogotá	Colombia	1.45
58	Kiev	Ukraine	1.45
58	Athens	Greece	1.45
58	Chisinau	Moldova	1.45
58	Beirut	Lebanon	1.45
58	Casablanca	Morocco	1.45
64	Mumbai	India	1.20
65	Jerusalem	Israel	1.09
65	Brussels	Belgium	1.09
65	Tallinn	Estonia	1.09
65	San Juan	Puerto Rico	1.09
65	Karachi	Pakistan	1.09
70	San Salvador	El Salvador	0.75
71	Ho Chi Minh City	Vietnam	0.73
71	Guayaquil	Ecuador	0.73
71	Quezon City	Philippines	0.73
71	Panama City	Panama	0.73
71	Santa Cruz	Bolivia	0.73
71	Caracas	Venezuela	0.73
71	Baku	Azerbaijan	0.73
78	Guatemala City	Guatemala	0.56
78	Dublin	Ireland	0.56

Table 9-1. *Continued*

Rank	City	Country	Participation
80	Lagos	Nigeria	0.36
80	Kuwait City	Kuwait	0.36
80	Sarajevo	Bosnia and Herzegovina	0.36
80	Nairobi	Kenya	0.36
84	Santo Domingo	Dominican Republic	0.00
84	Colombo	Sri Lanka	0.00
84	Kampala	Uganda	0.00
84	Tashkent	Uzbekistan	0.00

Table 9-2 represents the average score in Citizen Participation by continent. Overall, cities in Oceania ranked the highest among the continents with a score of 4.91, while cities in South America scored only 2.04 in this category. Oceania replaced Europe as the continent with the highest average, while South America replaced Africa as the continent with the lowest average score. Table 9-2 also presents the data separated by OECD and Non-OECD member countries for the category of Citizen Participation. Cities in OECD countries scored an average of 5.03, while cities in non-member countries scored only 2.77 in this category. This result indicates that cities in economically advanced countries continue to have more emphasis on citizen participation than do cities in less developed countries. Figures 9-1 and 9-2 illustrate the data presented in Table 9-2.

Table 9-2. *Average Score in Citizen Participation by Continent and OECD Member and Non-Member Countries (2009)*

	Oceania	Europe	Asia	Average	North America	Africa	South America
Participation Averages	4.91	3.89	3.78	3.50	3.40	2.54	2.04

Figure 9-1. *Average Score in Citizen Participation by Continent (2009)*

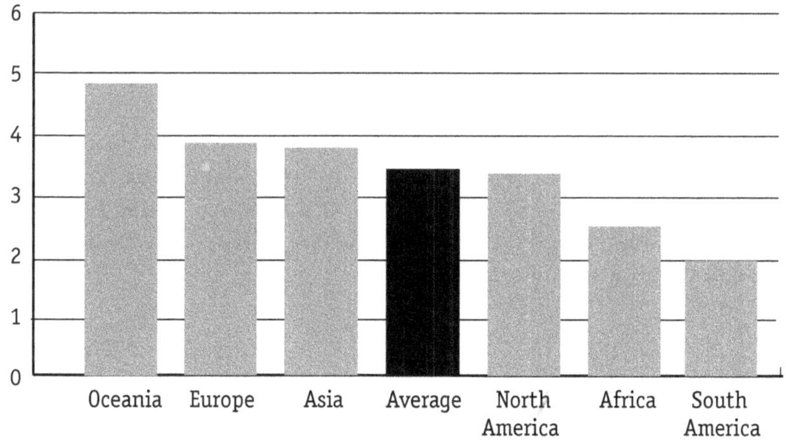

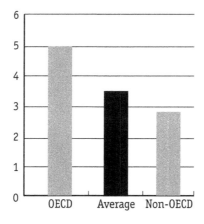

Figure 9-2. *Average Score in Citizen Participation by OECD Member and Non-Member Countries (2009)*

Table 9-3 indicates the results of key aspects selected for the category of Citizen Participation by continent. In terms of the evaluation of "Does the website allow users to provide comments or feedback to individual departments/agencies through online forms?," 70% of municipalities provide a mechanism allowing comments or feedback through online forms, compared to 64% in 2007. Fifty percent of cities in Oceania and much more in Europe, Asia, North America and South America provide such an online feedback form. With respect to online bulletin board or chat capabilities for gathering citizen input on public issues ("online bulletin board" or "chat capabilities" means the city website where any citizens can post ideas, comments, or opinions without specific discussion topics.), over 35% do have these capabilities. All cities in Oceania and 46% of cities in Europe provide online bulletin board or chat capabilities. With regard to online discussion forums on policy issues ("online discussion forum" means the city websites where the city arranges public consultation on policy issues and citizens participate in discussing those specific topics.), 33% of municipalities evaluated do have a site containing an online discussion forum, which increased from 21% in 2007. Additionally, the data from citywide performance measurement systems are being increasingly provided by the municipal websites for about 40% of the cities evaluated compared to only 20% in 2007. Oceanic and European cities lead the way with 100% and 71% of their cities currently offering such services.

Table 9-3. *Results for Citizen Participation by Continent (2009)*

	Oceania	Europe	Average	Asia	North America	South America	Africa
Feedback Form	50%	74%	70%	78%	78%	67%	33%
Bulletin Board	100%	46%	35%	35%	11%	22%	22%
Policy Forum	100%	43%	33%	22%	22%	11%	44%
Performance Measurement	100%	71%	40%	17%	22%	11%	11%

Table 9-4 represents the results of key aspects selected in the category of Citizen Participation by OECD membership. In terms of the evaluation of "Does the website allow users to provide comments or feedback to individual departments/agencies through online forms?," 82% of municipalities in OECD countries provide a mechanism allowing comments or feedback through online forms. About 64% of municipalities in non-OECD countries provide a mechanism allowing comments or feedback through online forms. With respect to online bulletin board or chat capabilities for gathering citizen input on public issues, 54% of municipalities in OECD countries provide online bulletin board or chat capabilities. Only 27% of municipalities in non-OECD countries provide online bulletin board or chat capabilities. With regard to online discussion forums on policy issues, 50% of municipalities in OECD countries have a site containing an online discussion forum. Only 25% of municipalities in non-OECD countries, however, have a site containing an online discussion forum. The data from citywide performance measurement systems are provided by 43% of municipalities in OECD countries, while about 39% of municipalities in non-OECD countries have performance measurement systems online. Figure 9-3 illustrates the overall presence of online policy forums.

Table 9-4. *Results for Citizen Participation by OECD Member and Non-Member Countries (2009)*

	OECD	Average	Non-OECD
Feedback Form	82%	70%	64%
Bulletin Board	54%	35%	27%
Policy Forum	50%	33%	25%
Performance Measurement	43%	40%	39%

Figure 9-3. *Online Policy Forums (2009)*

■ Online Policy Forum

▨ No Online Policy Forum

CHAPTER 10

Best Practices

Seoul

Overall, Seoul has been ranked #1 in this evaluation, just as it was in the 2007, 2005, and 2003 evaluations. Seoul has a well developed website that has recorded a high score in all five e-governance categories. It has been ranked the top city for 2009 in the areas of Content, Privacy, and Services. It was ranked second in Usability, and fourth in Citizen Participation.

Seoul's Cyber Policy Forum is representative of the municipality's efforts toward enhancing online citizen participation. The Cyber Policy Forum aims to "provide citizens with opportunities to understand policy issues and to facilitate discussions; to encourage citizen participation in public administration and to obtain feedback about policy issues; and to reflect citizens' opinions in city policies and produce more tailored policy solutions for citizens."

The website of Seoul provides a privacy policy that is accessible on every page that accepts data and addresses the use of cookies or web beacons to track users. The city's homepage is very user-friendly, along with targeted audience links available on each page. The city of Seoul continues to provide citizens with opportunities to participate in governmental processes, including well-organized and systematic opportunities to submit their ideas and suggestions on proposed policies via policy forums in which citizens can freely suggest policy ideas and agendas to public servants. The website is offered in more than one language—in Korean, English, Japanese, Chinese, French and Spanish.

Prague

The Prague municipal website has made great improvements over the past few years. Comparing the 2007 and 2009 evaluations, Prague leapt from 15th place to 2nd. Though Prague was ranked number 14 in 2005, it was not even ranked on the entire survey in 2003. This shows great effort on the part of city administrators to bring Prague up to good e-governance standards. Prague has a well-developed, aesthetically pleasing, and easily accessible website that has recorded a high score in all five e-governance categories. It has been ranked the first city for 2009 in Usability, and the second city in the areas of Citizen Participation and Privacy. It was ranked number six in Services, and number nine in Content.

Prague's website offers a detailed Privacy Policy, to which there is a link at the bottom of every page. The homepage provides targeted links, divided into detailed categories, for website visitors. For Usability, an excellent sitemap is provided, containing all active links in an easily viewable length of less than two screens. The website also offers an easily usable search function, complete with help and advanced search options, as well as the choice to limit searches to particular sections of the website. The site is regularly updated with interesting news and events. For Content, Prague especially excels in its supplying of a searchable database of e-mail addresses for administrator-contact capability. Furthermore, a searchable database of archives of public meeting minutes is provided. In the Services category, the Prague municipal website provides information for users to pay their utilities, allows users to download tax forms to print and return, includes information in real time for users who wish to track the progress of permits, and allows users not only to file complaints but to track their complaint as it is processed and/or action is taken. Prague particularly does well in Citizen Participation, providing the option to contact not only several departments through online forms, but also elected officials.

Hong Kong

The inclusion of Hong Kong as a best practice is based on its third place ranking in the 2009 evaluation. Hong Kong has consistently been a top ranked city in the Global E-Governance Survey since 2003. Hong Kong received an overall score of 61.51, which is not necessarily based on its best performance in any one category, but is, rather, a reflection of its balanced performance throughout all five categories. Hong Kong's ranking was second overall in 2003, after which it dropped slightly in 2005, but returned to second place in 2007. Hong Kong represents a model of consistency for other municipalities to aspire to, both in its evenly spread scores in individual categories, and its regular placing in the top four overall.

New York City

New York City increased its overall score from 2007 (56.54) to 2009 (62.83), and was ranked fifth or higher in the areas of Content and Service. New York City was the third ranked municipality in the area of Services. It has a website design formatted to encourage access to various municipal departments and the forms they provide. The New York City website provides extensive access to forms for permits, some of which can be filled out online. It also permits users to pay their utilities, taxes, fines, and tickets online, as well as providing bidders PDF forms to download and fill out for e-procurement. The city also provides an online form and email link so that users can submit complaints, plus a FAQ with several subcategories. Additionally, online forms to request information are provided. Finally, particularly impressive is that the municipal website contains online forms users can submit to report crimes, violations or corruption.

Singapore

The inclusion of Singapore as the fifth best practice for the 2009 report is based on its fifth place ranking in the 2009 evaluation. Singapore received an overall score of 56.81, a fall in performance from 2007, when it had an overall score of 68.56 and placed fourth. Singapore did well in all categories, balancing its performance. However, it showed particular achievement by placing second in the categories of Service and Usability, and sixth in Citizen Participation. The Singapore municipal website is well-formatted and easy to use, with consistent links, searchable databases, and a good sitemap.

For Services, the Singapore website provides extensive access to forms for permits, some of which can be filled out online. It also permits users to pay their utilities, taxes, fines, and tickets online. The city also provides an online form and email link so that users can submit complaints, plus a FAQ with several subcategories. Additionally, online forms to request information are provided. The website encourages Citizen Participation through online bulletin boards and surveys. The website also allows users to register or purchase tickets to events in city/municipal halls, arenas or other facilities of the city.

CHAPTER 11

Conclusion

The study of municipal e-governance practices throughout the world is an area that clearly requires ongoing research. Our research represents a continued effort to evaluate digital governance in large municipalities throughout the world. Previous research on government websites has focused primarily on e-governance at the federal, state, and local levels in the United States. Only a few studies have produced comparative analyses of e-governance in national governments throughout the world. Our studies in 2003, 2005, 2007 and 2009 have produced findings that contribute to the e-governance literature, in particular in the areas of website Privacy/Security, Usability, Content, Services, and Citizen Participation. The 2009 study highlights the increased attention spent on Privacy and Security, Content and Services, and the need for further attention in the area of Usability and Citizen Participation via municipal websites. Similar to our previous findings, citizen participation has recorded the lowest score among the five categories. Cities are yet to recognize the importance of involving and supporting citizen participation online. A promising finding in terms of citizen participation, however, is the growing tendency among municipalities to publish performance measurement data on their websites. The number of websites providing data from citywide performance measurement systems has doubled globally in 2007.

In addition, the digital gap between OECD and non-OECD member countries in average scores that increased in 2005 had decreased slightly in 2007 and continued to decrease in 2009. It is very important for international organizations such as the UN and cities in advanced countries to help continue bridging the digital divide. In many nations, especially those belonging to the non-OECD category, the digital divide may imply more than access to the internet alone; this divide refers to access to basic infrastructure such telephones, electricity, communications, etc. We therefore recommend developing a comprehensive policy for bridging that divide. That comprehensive policy should include capacity building for municipalities, including information infrastructure, content, applications and access for individuals and educating the residents with appropriate computer education.

The continued study of municipalities worldwide, with a fourth evaluation planned in 2011, will further provide insights into the direction of e-governance and the performance of e-governance throughout regions of the world.

Every region has examples of best practices for overall performance and in each specific e-governance category. As municipalities seek to increase their municipal website performance, searching for models within their region is an opportunity to identify e-governance benchmarks. Those municipalities that serve as top performers in their respective regions can then look to the top ranked cities in municipalities throughout the world. Although the 2009 study highlights increases in e-governance performance throughout the world, continuous improvement should be the norm for every municipality.

BIBLIOGRAPHY

Giga Consulting. (2000). Scorecard Analysis of the New Jersey Department of Treasury. An unpublished report to the NJ Department of Treasury.

Holzer, M, & Kim, S.T., (2003) "Digital Governance in Municipalities Worldwide, A Longitudinal Assessment of Municipal Web Sites Throughout the World", the E-Governance Institute, Rutgers University, Newark and the Global e-policy e-government Institute, Sungkyunkwan, University.

Holzer, M, & Kim, S.T., (2005) "Digital Governance in Municipalities Worldwide, A Longitudinal Assessment of Municipal Web Sites Throughout the World", the E-Governance Institute, Rutgers University, Newark and the Global e-policy e-government Institute, Sungkyunkwan, University

Holzer, M, & Kim, S.T., (2007) "Digital Governance in Municipalities Worldwide, A Longitudinal Assessment of Municipal Web Sites Throughout the World", the E-Governance Institute, Rutgers University, Newark and the Global e-policy e-government Institute, Sungkyunkwan, University

Howard, M. (2001). e-Government across the globe: How will "e" change Government? *Government Finance Review,* (August) 6-9.

Kaylor, C. et al. 2001. "Gauging e-government: A report on implementing services among American cities." *Government Information Quarterly* 18: 293-307.

Melitski, J., Holzer, M., Kim, S.-T., Kim, C.-G., & Rho, SY. (2005) Digital Government Worldwide: An e-Government Assessment of Municipal Web-sites. *International Journal of E-Government Research.* 1(1) 01-19.

Moon, M. Jae. 2002. "The evolution of E-government among municipalities: Rhetoric or reality?" *Public Administration Review* 62(4): 424-433.

Moon, M. Jae, and P. deLeon. 2001. "Municipal Reinvention: Municipal Values and Diffusion among Municipalities." *Journal of Public Administration Research and Theory* 11(3): 327-352.

Musso, J. et. al. 2000. "Designing Web Technologies for Local Governance Reform: Good Management or Good Democracy." *Political Communication* 17(l): 1-19.

Pardo, T. (2000). *Realizing the promise of digital government: It's more than building a web site.* Albany, NY: Center for Technology in Government.

Weare, C. et al. 1999. "Electronic Democracy and the Diffusion of Municipal Web Pages in California." *Administration and Society* 31(1): 3-27.

West, D. M. 2001—2005. *Global E-Government Survey,* Available at http://www. insidepolitics.org/ Accessed March 16, 2006.

APPENDIX

PRIVACY/ SECURITY

1-2. A privacy or security statement/policy

3-6. Data collection

7. Option to have personal information used

8. Third party disclosures

9. Ability to review personal data records

10. Managerial measures

11. Use of encryption

12. Secure server

13. Use of "cookies" or "Web Beacons"

14. Notification of privacy policy

15. Contact or e-mail address for inquiries

16. Public information through a restricted area

17. Access to nonpublic information for employees

18. Use of digital signatures

USABILITY

19-20. Homepage, page length.

21. Targeted audience

22-23. Navigation Bar

24. Site map

25-27. Font Color

30-31. Forms

32-37. Search tool

38. Update of website

CONTENT

39. Information about the location of offices

40. Listing of external links

41. Contact information

42. Minutes of public

43. City code and regulations

44. City charter and policy priority

45. Mission statements

46. Budget information

47-48. Documents, reports, or books (publications)

49. GIS capabilities

50. Emergency management or alert mechanism

51-52. Disability access

53. Wireless technology

54. Access in more than one language

55-56. Human resources information

57. Calendar of events

58. Downloadable documents

SERVICE

59-61. Pay utilities, taxes, fines

62. Apply for permits

63. Online tracking system

64-65. Apply for licenses

66. E-procurement

67. Property assessments

68. Searchable databases

69. Complaints

70-71. Bulletin board about civil applications

72. FAQ

73. Request information

74. Customize the main city homepage

75. Access private information online

76. Purchase tickets

77. Webmaster response

78. Report violations of administrative laws and regulations

CITIZEN PARTICIPATION

79-80. Comments or feedback

81-83. Newsletter

84. Online bulletin board or chat capabilities

85-87. Online discussion forum on policy issues

88-89. Scheduled e-meetings for discussion

90-91. Online survey/polls

92. Synchronous video

93-94. Citizen satisfaction survey

95. Online decision-making

96-98. Performance measures, standards, or benchmarks

www.ingramcontent.com/pod-product-compliance
Lightning Source LLC
Chambersburg PA
CBHW061020050326

40689CB00012B/2692